MW01286541

CAMPING IS FOR EVERYONE

A GUIDE TO ENJOYING THE OUTDOORS

JONATHAN L. WESTON

Camping is for Everyone
A Guide to Enjoying the Outdoors

Copyright © 2022 by Jonathan L. Weston

ISBN 978-0-578-38485-6

Published by:

The OBA Group
Atlanta GA 30326

THIS BOOK IS DEDICATED TO MY CHILDREN.
THE MANY NIGHTS UNDER THE STARS I'VE SPENT,
NOT ONE HAS PASSED WITHOUT THOUGHTS OF YOU.

LOVE,
YOUR FATHER

CONTENTS

AUTHORS NOTE

Thank you so much for reading, *Camping is for Everyone*. As my campground, Wanderland, which is located in North Georgia, grew in popularity with new campers every week, I found that I was asked similar questions such as; "What should we bring camping?" "What size tent should we buy?" "Can I bring my dog camping?"

Many people knew how much time I spent in the forest, but most didn't know about the project that was underway. For years, I would research a new topic with each excursion and every weekend another bushcraft skill was explored.

However, The original story was not nearly as camping-focused. Since I was writing as I was living, the original version of this book would sometimes wander (which contributed to the name of the campground I founded; Wanderland). I drifted into my personal thoughts, where I was in life, and what I wanted in my future. There were directions I expected this story to go in, things I had to heal from, that I realized just didn't belong in this editorial work. This book allowed me to focus on just camping and correctly add elements of the camping experience that will give the first-time camper a much better impact and reader experience.

I thank all my sources of learning and knowledge. I am a student of the outdoors and still learning along my journey.

I hope this book aids the millions of first-time campers who don't know where to start.

In this book, I share the essentials needed to have a great time in the woods with your family and friends. As this is an introductory book on camping. There is much more to learn. As you explore, never stop learning, never stop asking questions and never think that camping just isn't for you.

Thank you so much for purchasing this book and your dedication to better understanding the outdoors. Camping is for everyone.

Enjoy!
Jonathan L. Weston

PREFACE

Why did I write this book? I asked myself that question many times as this love story with the outdoors began to unfold. I had just moved to Atlanta. I was working, dating, and getting to know the city. Professionally recovering and re-evaluating the importance of all things presented to me. I was just trying to be ok with missing my children and all the guilt associated with deciding to survive after a rough divorce. It seemed my life was not going how I imagined it. Would I ever be able to love again? Would I ever feel happy again? These thoughts weighed on me constantly. They undulated through my day with reckless abandon and malice. I needed quiet. I needed to process. I needed to accept it. I needed to surrender. I needed the forest.

Early in my divorce, my good friend Reese Bessinger from Columbia, South Carolina, invited me to go hunting with him. He had seen some rather emotional internet messages authored by me and being a good friend, he reached out. I accepted the invitation, and a few weeks later, I found myself in a tree stand at 4 in the morning, looking at a perfectly round and glowing moon. For the first time in a long time, I felt at peace. I felt at home in the cold; I felt safe with my rifle in my hand. I could feel something good again. I was hooked on the crisp air and silence. Since that time, there was a constant draw to the darkest parts of the forest. But I didn't know everything I needed to know to survive in the woods. I would go too deep in for too long and push my abilities with each outing. It was really not a good way of learning. I needed to understand the fundamentals.

That fact was never more evident than the night I found myself alone in the middle of the forest. I had walked further than I thought and longer than I could remember. I walked like I had no plans to come back. The sun had set, and the nocturnal residents moved about. But I, a visitor to the woods, was vibrating and on edge. Every movement screamed for my attention. Every sound-triggered my fight or flight reflex. I was afraid. I was unprotected. Most importantly, I was lost.

That night I sat there under a tree; my eyes had been retrained to see after a few hours of darkness. The forest seemed bright by this point and I was thankful for the moon's illumination. Hours before, I had stopped moving, opting to instead wait till daybreak to find my path out of the forest. In life and navigating the woods, it's not where you are that matters; it's understanding how you got there.

I sat under that tree and decided that I would learn enough about the outdoors to never again find myself in the same predicament. That's where this project began. In this book, you will learn the basics that will get you started. Enjoy the outdoors. Camping is for everyone.

CAMPING IS FOR EVERYONE

"Wilderness is not a luxury but a necessity of the human spirit."
— Edward Abbey

What are you into? What experience is most beneficial to your day? There are many ways to enjoy a day or weekend of camping.

In this book, we will introduce novice campers to what they need to know to successfully navigate most basic camping trips. Camping gives everyone the chance to experience wildlife firsthand. Campers usually can engage in hunting, fishing, plant study, swimming, canoeing, nature photography, and wildlife watching. Or take a lot of pictures outside. There isn't a wrong way to enjoy the outdoors. Camping is for everyone.

While camping is for everyone, there is an inherent danger the further we venture into the wild. Knowledge of the outdoors will keep you and your family safe. Here are a few stats:

- Camping steadily grew in popularity before 2020 but experienced aggressive growth across the U.S. The 2021 North American Camping Report, which surveyed U.S. and Canadian campers' sentiments and behaviors on outdoor recreation in January 2021, shows that more than 86 million U.S. households consider themselves campers, and 48 million of those households took at least one camping trip in 2020 – up more than 6 million over 2019.

- 56% of campers are Millennials.

- Over the last couple of years, 40 million people have taken RV trips.

- Campers are also more diverse than ever as the incidence of camping among non-white and same-sex communities meets or exceeds national representation. 60% of first-time campers in 2020 represent diverse ethnic groups, while 61% of same-sex households camp with children, an increase of 12 percentage points over 2019.

- Every year 1 million new families in the U.S. start camping. This number has been increasing every year since 2020. 81% of campers say their main goal is to spend time with their family and friends.

- The top five words associated with this industry are Outdoors (89%), Campfire (89%), Fun (84%), Tent (83%), and Adventure (80%).

- On average, trips are planned 25 days in advance.

- Twenty-one percent of the 48 million households who camped at least once in 2020 classified themselves as first-time campers. This equates to 10.1 million households in 2020 and is a significant increase compared to 4% of new campers in 2019.

- These first-time campers are under 40, parents, and ethnically diverse. More than half stayed at campgrounds with at least some amenities and services and purchased some camping gear for their first trip. Nearly half tried glamping, and 28% identified as RV campers.

- First-time campers said that having access to technology allowed them to camp an additional nine days in 2020.

Of the first-time campers who indicated having a "great" first experience in 2020, nearly 75% claim they are likely to continue camping. The factors that contributed to campers having an enjoyable experience, and could contribute to other first-timers having a positive camping trip in 2021, include:

1. Having an existing love of the outdoors and a desire to try camping.

2. A pleasant, low maintenance experience at a campground that included many services and amenities (such as bathrooms and showers, on-site activities, a campground store, Wi-Fi, and more.

3. Sharing the experience with friends or as part of a bigger group.

This surge in popularity compels us to educate anyone who wants to know more about the outdoors. Camping delivers many physical and mental health benefits: the fresh air, open space, outdoor activities, and camping builds confidence in children and offers the opportunity for adult campers to challenge themselves with figuring out the outdoors. In this book, we will give you the ideas and framework to prepare yourself for a great day outside. But you will grow in your personal comfort and confidence with each outdoor excursion.

SOME OF THE MANY BENEFITS OF CAMPING

As detailed in the previous chapter, more and more people are discovering the benefits of camping and spending time outdoors. "Why? What's the draw?," you may ask.

Camping offers so many benefits to your well-being. It's good for you, both in body and mind. Benefits include relationship building, opportunities to learn and develop new skills, unplugging and getting away from screens, connecting with nature, stress reduction, and increasing physical fitness. The fitness benefits of camping are also well documented. Research suggests that physical activity outdoors and feelings of connection to nature enhance psychological health and well-being. Activities such as walking in forests and participating in outdoor activities, have enhanced mood and focus, and increased attention and cognitive capacity. Additionally, significant improvements in self-esteem occur with physical activity in the great outdoors. The physical demands of backpacking, setting up tents and making camp, hiking, fishing, and exploring nature count as exercise, contributing to our overall health and well-being. Outdoor physical activity has been linked to decreased depressive thoughts. Sleeping under the stars can help promote our natural circadian rhythm, the foundation for high-quality sleep and health.

We all know that camping can be a relaxing escape from the daily grind. You can bathe in the forest, trading the sound of traffic for the songs of the wind, water, bugs, and birds while creating memories with your friends and family. But beyond that, your body needs it. Your soul needs it. You need it. You need to go camping for specific reasons you may not have considered. The benefits of camping are endless, but these might be the most compelling.

Clean Air

Whether or not you live in a city, there's a good chance that the air you're breathing every day isn't exactly fresh. The United States Environmental Protection Agency (EPA) has identified air pollution as one of the primary causes of asthma and other breathing-related issues affecting nearly 30 million people in the United States alone.

The Environmental Pollution journal makes the case that being in trees and natural wilderness (as most of us are when we're camping for a weekend) improves air quality far beyond what a cleaner can do in an urban or nature-depleted environment. In short, your lungs are craving the campground.

Your Circadian Rhythm

With the right gear and preparation, camping can actually improve your sleep quality and your natural circadian rhythm. Our circadian rhythms are consistently thrown off by the presence of electricity, digital devices, and inconsistent sleep patterns. In fact, as the National Sleep Foundation attests, only 1 in 10 Americans list sleep as a priority among other commitments such as fitness and nutritional health. Yet, among working adults, sleep has a documented impact on both personal achievement and overall happiness. Over 65% of adults admit that their effectiveness depends on how much sleep they're getting.

Our recommendation: don't skimp on the sleeping gear. Especially if you're car camping, don't be afraid to bring that inflatable mattress or a couple of sleeping pads to stack on top of each other. Once you've nailed down your cozy requirements, indulge in a night of sleep in the (relative) solitude of the outdoors. You'll be amazed at what a couple nights unhindered by the blue light of a computer or television screen will do for your body and mind.

Stress Relief

Fortunately, one of the most valuable benefits of camping is that you don't have to work too hard to achieve peace and stress relief. The American Institute of Stress reported that over 60% of Americans claim that work-related stress was the most common source of angst in their lives. Second, only to money and the future of America, it's clear that the workweek, even at the most successful of companies, takes a toll on the human psyche.

Whether or not you love your job, ignoring the chronic stress that arises from life's mundane commitments (bills, etc.) can be detrimental to your mental, physical, and emotional health. Though not a replacement for a therapist, a camping trip can do wonders for the stress levels in the body. It allows you ample opportunities to escape the bind of schedules, itineraries, and required tasks, allowing you to refocus on the important things in life. For instance, such things as: fishing, hiking , or most importantly, building a campfire and then doing nothing at all.

Dopamine

The science of dopamine shows us that it's easy to get caught in artificial dopamine-feedback loops, where our brains are trained to adapt to habits that aren't necessarily helpful or healthy. Whether it's due to work, a dependency on technology, social media addiction, or the desire to unwind at the end of a long day, we can damage our dopamine receptors simply by remaining unchanged in our sedentary habits. The human body craves movement and nature to refresh its capacity for memory, mindfulness, and overall energy levels. One of the benefits of camping is that it helps to retrain those neurotransmitters by reinforcing healthy habits like hiking, meditating, or simply spending time connected to nature. Humans are biologically wired to crave natural scenery, so a weekend-long camping trip will do wonders for your soul and brain.

Reducing Inflammation

Recent medical studies have shown that inflammation levels in the body have risen at alarming rates in the last 15-20 years, particularly in the United States.

Although there are a variety of causes for this (including genetics), a primary trigger is an unhealthy lifestyle and diet. Camping is scientifically proven to reduce oxidative stress. It encourages an active lifestyle and reduces your level of exposure to environmental pollutants, which are a key factor in developing free radicals that cause oxidative cell damage. Being outside consistently and avoiding the city for a weekend helps your body recover from stress symptoms while also reducing the levels of inflammation throughout your system.

"You Time "

Whether or not we admit it, everyone needs the time and space to become self-aware. Frankly, the opportunities to do that in the modern world are scarce.

In an article in The Atlantic in 2017, California State Polytechnic University sociologist, Jack Fong, asserts that the value of solitude, while stigmatized in modern society, can actually be an important part of developing positive psychological patterns. "For Fong, who meditates 15 minutes a day and takes monthly solo camping trips, it is at least as essential as exercise or healthy eating. Possibly, he says, it is necessary for a truly healthy mind. 'It really lifts you out of problems. It really has a powerful function for making you understand your predicament in this universe,' he says."

As Fong attests, camping, especially solo camping (if you're game), can function as a self-care retreat. You can truly process and ponder the things weighing on both your mind and body. At a loss for how to treat yourself to a dose of the outdoors? Try hiking or visiting a quiet trail for a meditative walk through the woods.

Vitamin D

Recent research suggests that vitamin D deficiency affects over 40% of Americans. If you live in a region where seasonal weather is especially varied, you're among this growing number of Americans. Commonly associated with sunshine, Vitamin D plays a key role in helping the body absorb calcium, which promotes strong bone growth and helps maintain healthy cells. While the body makes Vitamin D on its own, it only does so after your skin absorbs enough sunlight. Getting outdoors can benefit your overall health. Vitamin D combined with natural light can increase your energy while stabilizing your vision, mind, and overall stress levels. Particularly after a long week at work or after the often cloudy winter season, camping can be a great way to replenish your body's critical vitamin D levels.

Touch the Earth

In an article published in the Journal of Environmental and Public Health, researchers suggest that grounding oneself can benefit both psychological well-being and overall health. It's not so much the feeling of it that's healthy, but the fact that the Earth contains an infinitely self-replenishing supply of free electrons, which have the potential to establish a "stable internal bioelectrical environment for the normal functioning of all body systems."

Whether it's relaxation, energy, or both, camping is the perfect time to appreciate the wild with nothing but your bare soles. Go ahead. Get your feet wet.

Reconnect

While not all camping trips are helpful for those keeping to a strict diet, camping can be a great time to get back in touch with your nutritional values. Whether through foraging for your own food or creating your own plant-based recipes, the outdoors is a prime place to invest in a fresh, new lifestyle and stabilize your gut health. Eating fresh and plant-based foods while outdoors can increase vitamin D levels and reduce stress. A significant cause of physical stress is linked to diets high in carbohydrates, processed sugars, and alcohol.

Forest Bathing

Meditation not your thing? Try forest bathing. Studies that have been conducted for years in the Eastern world attest to the benefits of the regular practice of forest bathing. The execution of the concept is quite simple: take a short, relaxed walk through the woods or a densely natured area, and wait for nature to do its thing. After some time alone, chances are you'll feel recharged and ready to jump back into your normal activities. Take your nature walk on bare feet and get grounded as you bathe in the forest air!

Exercise

A camping trip that combines exercise with being outdoors will improve your overall well-being. Although most adults agree that exercise is a priority, most working Americans admit that work, family, and day-to-day exhaustion often make regular fitness a non-reality. Even if you're already a fitness junkie, getting away from the treadmill and outdoors for a trail run or a hike will add much-needed variety to your exercise routine.

Disconnect

It is becoming increasingly clear that the amount of technology we're confronted with daily affects our short-term memory and our ability to interact with others. Blue lights from screens interrupt circadian rhythms. The constant influx of notifications is listed as one of the top sleep disruptors.

Camping provides a respite from technology in a way that encourages physical activity, overall health, and human connection.

Not sure you can last a whole weekend without your device or have a family member you need to keep in touch with? Try a daily "check-in" time (preferably limited to around 20 minutes). You can keep tabs on your email, check-in with a friend, answer a call or two, then put the phone away for the day. If you're an avid music listener, try downloading your tunes in advance and placing your device on airplane mode.

Expand

Maybe you haven't camped in 20 years, or camping was never really on your radar. Whether you're experienced or a newbie in the outdoors, camping allows you to stretch out of your comfort zone in one way or another. Whether through taking that long hike you've been dreading or cooking your own fresh-caught fish over a campfire.

You'll find yourself invigorated by the challenges and inspired to do more in the outdoors or even in your day-to-day life.

Get Creative

If you feel like your job (or life in general) puts pressure on you to be more productive than creative, you're not alone. Many people think they are not living up to their creative potential. But here's some good news. There isn't much to get done once you've set up camp and built a fire. But have you ever had a tent pole break in the middle of setting it up or lost the only lighter you brought along? And if a tent pole breaks in the middle of setting it up or you misplace a lighter you brought along, here's your chance to flex those creative muscles.

Unexpected events happen outdoors, and camping encourages us to get creative with our limited options and gear. Whether solving a problem or coming up with a new game to play that doesn't involve a screen, camping is an excellent way to get your creative juices flowing. You might even find that creativity blends into your personal or work life as well, as your brain subconsciously unwinds the threads of problems you've been working to solve.

Get Perspective

Camping has the power to allow you space to get perspective on your life and priorities by giving you space and time away from distractions. In the ordinary world, it's easy to distract yourself from focusing on what's most important to you, whether through work, electronics, or social events. Taking time away from your office, technology, your household responsibilities, and even social pressures can do wonders for helping you prioritize your life.

Suppose you've found yourself at a loss for your next step or in a funk with work, friends, and life. In that case, a weekend getaway should be on the top of your list for things that could help you gain significant and much-needed perspective.

Why wouldn't you want to go camping with all of these health benefits?

WAYS TO CAMP

"Is that weird, taking my Louis Vuitton bag camping?"
— Jessica Simpson

No Jessica... it's not! This chapter will explore some popular ways to get outside and go camping. There are many ways one can get outside. There isn't a wrong way. Camping is for everyone.

DAY HIKING

Day hiking is becoming more popular with campers of all ages. Anyone capable of walking long distances can do this. A day hikers' objective is to hike or walk for the day and return to the place of origin that same day, usually, as night approaches their campsite. Besides being able to walk long distances, you must also be ready for any weather conditions and have the right tools and techniques to find the correct route back to your campsite.

One crucial thing in hiking is selecting the proper footwear. You will be "on your feet," so you must purchase footwear explicitly designed for hiking that primarily keeps your feet comfortable while walking. Never buy footwear solely based on how good they look. It's about protecting your feet. Protection from the elements is always an important consideration when selecting the right shoe.

Choosing the Right Shoe

Where Will You Be Hiking?

There is going out for a "casual" hike where the trails are cleared and easy to navigate. Then there is "HIKING"! In this second version, your shoe must be really thought through based on the terrain you may encounter. How rough will the terrain be? Hills? Stoney trails? No trails at all?

Different environments mean you need to consider other types of hiking boots to fit the conditions. Lightweight boots are more suitable for everyday hiking. More supportive and waterproof hiking boots will usually be better if you're hiking on rough terrain or cutting new paths.

What's the weather like when you go hiking? Do you mostly go hiking in hot, dry, and dusty conditions? Or will you be hiking in cold climates? What sort of weather conditions you'll be hiking in will help narrow down the features you need in your hiking boots. If hiking in wet and cold conditions, waterproof hiking boots are essential. If hiking through the bush or in hot conditions, a breathable boot is more important to avoid excess moisture in your boots.

How Long Will You Be Hiking For?

The duration of your hikes is another consideration when choosing the proper hiking boots. Of course, sometimes you may hike for longer or shorter, but think about whether you'll be going on hikes for a few hours, a full day, or hike over several days or even weeks. The longer you plan to hike, the more supportive your hiking boots need to be. Longer hikes usually mean you'll be carrying more gear, so your shoes will need extra support for the excess weight you'll be carrying. For longer hikes, make sure your boots are durable and don't forget to break them in before setting off on your hiking adventure.

What Type of Fit Do You Need?
In terms of hiking boots, fit comes down to 3 key factors – length, weight, and volume. For length, make sure you can wiggle your toes inside the boot. Your feet shouldn't slide around inside the boot with regard to width. Equally, they shouldn't be so tight that they are compressed from the sides. Volume refers to how much space your foot takes up inside the boot. Your foot should feel secure inside the boot but not too tight. Also, consider the arch support available in the boot. If you have high arches and plan long hiking trips, it may be worth speaking to a podiatrist about custom orthotics. These points will help you avoid unnecessary pain and blistering from poor-fitting hiking boots.

Many are attracted to this "sport" because every individual sets their own objective then strives hard to achieve it; this undertaking requires some commitment and planning.

BACKPACKING CAMPING

Backpacking is generally the most exciting and basic way of experiencing a wilderness adventure. Backpacking adds new excitement and elements to any hiking experience because it extends your visit in the backwoods. You may travel far into the wilderness because you are not obliged to go back to your campsite at the day's end. Everything you need for your journey is in your backpack and you travel with it.

Backpacking is simply exploring beautiful and wild country on foot. Being self-sufficient, while hiking with camping essentials in a comfortable backpack and setting up a camp mostly in undeveloped and primitive areas is a very exhilarating experience.

Put simply, backpacking entails having to carry a pack of essential camping supplies on your "back." However, keep in mind that the longer your trip, the more supplies you will have to carry. And what you decide to take along with you, as well as the distance you will hike is totally up to you.

Preparing for your backpacking trip involves assembling, selecting and packing supplies and gear that you need and want to bring.

Selecting your backpacking gear is very significant to have a successful trip. Excessive gear or specifically the wrong kind of backpacking gear can bring about a hefty weight load that will spoil your hike. Likewise, incorrect or too little gear will result in discomfort and under certain conditions, may even be dangerous.

The selections for backpacking gear are always evolving, ongoing and constantly changing. Backpacking equipment generally costs more compared to car camping, however much less compared to RV camping.

Here we must introduce the gear you bring into the woods. It will all fall within the guides of the 5 C's of bushcraft. What are the five C's? These are the primary categories that organize the basis of what it takes to survive in the outdoors. The five C's of bushcraft survivability are:

1. Covering - Protection of your body, clothing, boots, tents, bug spray, anything that protects your body from the elements.

2. Cutlery - Primarily your knife, but also your hatchet, axes or any other tool sharpened for purpose.

3. Combustion - This category encompasses starting a fire and creating light.

4. Cordage - These are bindings, cords, or any rope you can use for hanging a tent, bear bag, or making a tourniquet. Rope or string is important to keep in the pack.

5. Containers - Containers are anything that stores your food, water, or gear. (your actual backpack should be considered essential gear and belongs in this category)

TENT CAMPING

Tent camping is where skills are tested and what many would call the most authentic camping experience. Tent camping many times combines hiking and backpacking. It's usually combined with an overnight adventure in the woods. Tent camping may seem too daunting to try if you're a beginner or even worse, if faced by extremities such as sudden rainfall, strong winds and so on. Having a grasp on basic knowledge on the whole procedure can greatly help in lessening the effects of most of these challenges.

With regular practice and strict adherence to the basic steps and tips below, setting up camping tents won't be as daunting.

A properly set up tent will protect you against winds, rain and/or any other outdoor nuisances for a relaxing night's sleep.

Below are the steps you should follow when setting up a tent.

Step 1: Setting the Tent's Foundation

The first step is to lay out the tent's footprint by laying a protective tarp or groundsheet on the ground. The tarp provides a barrier between the base of the tent and the ground. It protects the tent from gathering moisture from underneath thus improving the tent's overall lifespan.

The tarp also assists in smoothing out the ground for extra comfort and keeps the tent base clean from dirt, wetness or dust when packing. If the footprint is larger than the floor of the tent, make sure to tuck the visible edges beneath. This ensures that water collected by the rainfly doesn't get underneath the tent base over the tarp.

Step 2: Roll Out the Tent Atop of the Foundation

Unfold the tent, identify the base of the tent and lay that side on top of the tarp or groundsheet taking into account where you want the door to be. The direction of the door will be especially important to factor in when using a bigger tent as it will be difficult to reposition it once set up.

Separate out the tent poles and fly, and ready the pegs/ stakes for use. Keep a record of the number of tent pegs to counter-check when packing.

Step 3: Connecting the Tent Poles

Tent poles are usually in bits that are linked together with a stretchy cord or bungee ropes to make them foldable and easier to store. Prepare the tent poles by connecting the various sections and lay them out across the flat tent. Refer to the instructions manual or attach the poles with corresponding numbers or colors, otherwise you may label them for more ease next time.

The interlinked sections of the tent poles are going to be connected using a push action instead of a pull action. Pulling may detach the tent poles and lead to more frustrations when setting up the tent. Most tents require only two tent poles crossing each other to form an X as part of the frame. But remember to push them through the connections rather than trying to pull them.

Some tents will require you to connect to the outer fly before clipping in the inner side. In this case place the ends of the poles into the pole attachments. Bend the poles to fit them in place and lastly clip the top and sides of the inner tent onto the poles.

On the other hand, other tents have sleeves/flaps as opposed to having clips to connect the poles. Simply slide the tent poles through the sleeves then secure the pole ends into the attachments at the base of the tent. Some tents also have a tie at the peak of the inner tent to keep the poles intact with the top with a simple bow.

Step 4: Staking in the Tent

Staking your tent holds the tent and anything else inside, in one place in case of sudden gusts of wind. Ensure the door is facing the right direction, away from the wind's direction, before staking the tent. If it isn't, simply turn the tent and tarp to the right direction. The poles for a self-standing tent will bend in place to raise the tent itself while in a regular tent you may be required to slowly bend the poles and then raise the tent in place.

Use a peg/stake to secure the four tent corners to the ground. Add some tension on the tent by pulling the corners away from each other to remove any slack before placing the stakes or pegs. The stakes should be pushed far enough into the ground and at a 45% angle leaning away from the tent.

The stakes should be exposed enough for easy removal when taking down and adequate for slipping a tie-down cord over them. A large rock, mallet or hammer can help drive the stakes/pegs into the ground. Always pack extra stakes as a precautionary measure.

Step 5: Attaching the Rainfly
Place the rain fly over the top of the tent frame and align the fly's door with the door of the inner tent. Use the loops or tabs on the inside of the rainfly to secure it to the poles and ensure the fly's doors are zipped closed.

Stake the fly in place, by drawing the bottom loops of the fly as far away from the inner tent as possible. Make sure to maintain an even tension across the fly to avoid it from flapping or touching the inner tent. This will make it more effective in airflow management and protecting the inner tent from any elements. Rain may stretch out the fly's material thus you need to recheck and readjust the fly's tension regularly.

Step 6: Guying Out the Tent
The last step is on securing your shelter to the ground or to nearby logs, rocks or trees. Guylines create extra tension across the tent thus creating more stability of the tent against high winds and so on. The guylines also help in keeping the fly away from the inner tent thus improving on air ventilation in the tent.

Guylines are attached at the guyout points on the side of the tent that the wind is coming from, however the guyout points can be added evenly around the tent for equal stabilization on all sides.

A trekking pole can also be used if there's no tree or rock nearby. Try to maintain the guylines perpendicular to the respective guyout points for increased tent strength. Notably, non-freestanding tents can't stand without the use of guylines.

GLAMPING

Some call it luxury camping. Some call it glamorous camping. Many only "glamp" some won't ever. It's all up to your preferences, there is no wrong way.

Glamping is a portmanteau of "glamorous" and "camping", and describes a style of camping with amenities and, in some cases, resort-style services not usually associated with "traditional" camping. Glamping has become particularly popular with 21st century tourists seeking the luxuries of hotel accommodation alongside the escapism and adventure recreation of camping.

Glamping is where stunning nature meets modern luxury. Experiential travel is an authentic way to connect with nature. Together, the experience is about stepping off the beaten path, walking away from superficial tourist activities and embracing an immersive cultural environment. By pushing themselves out of their comfort zones, experiential travelers experience a shift in perspective that improves the way they connect with the world. This transformational style of travel will enrich a person's life and, ultimately, leave an impression that lasts much longer than the journey itself.

BEACH CAMPING

As with any camping trip, you're going to need the basics. Tent, tarp, sleeping bag, cooking tools… you know the drill. One helpful trick of the trade that applies especially well to beach camping? Bring along a dustpan and brush. You'll be happy that you did when you're able to brush off the sand and keep your sleeping quarters clean. Another helpful piece of gear are sand stakes. These handy little tools are meant to hold their ground in loose surfaces, saving you a lot of potential tent frustration.

Get ready for the sun

Because beaches, by their nature, tend to be alongside expansive bodies of water, you're going to want to prepare yourself for the glaring sun that will inevitably reflect off the waves. If you've managed to secure a site with shade, amazing. If not, plan ahead. If you have the luxury of a car, consider adding a beach umbrella to your gear stash. It'll be indispensable when the midday sun is beating down on you and you've got nowhere else to go. It's also incredibly important to remember sunscreen and wide-brimmed hats. Nothing ruins a camping trip faster than a bad sunburn.

Understand the tide

This one is applicable if you're setting up camp beside the ocean and while it's probably pretty obvious, it absolutely bears repeating. Before pitching your tent and building your bonfire, be absolutely positive that you are well away from the reaches of the water when it hits high tide. Familiarize yourself with the tides ahead of time and organize yourself accordingly. It may be tempting to set up shop right near the water but you'll be singing a different tune when all your possessions are washed away after a particular aggressive wave.

Shelter

Even the most devoted sun worshippers can use a break every so often. And most of us can agree that some foods just taste better if they haven't been sitting under powerful rays all morning. If you have the space, consider taking along a collapsible sun shelter which, in addition to providing some welcome shade, can be used as a refuge from mosquitoes and rain. Most sun shelters come with removable screen walls and are tall roomy enough to accommodate several campers, making them the ideal place to come together for meals, games of cards, or just breezy naps.

Sand dunes

While they may be pretty to look at, sand dunes tend to house vulnerable vegetation that are easily (and negatively) affected by human interference. Additionally, they pose a risk as they are covered with shifting sand and rocks that can quickly slide down, creating a dangerous environment for everyone involved. Feel free to admire the dunes and marvel at their general awesomeness but for their sake and yours, keep your hands, feet, and everything else to yourself.

Moisture

Even though the days may be hot and sunny, nights spent by the water tend to get foggy and damp pretty quickly. Before turning in for the night, pack away anything you'd prefer to keep dry and be sure to set up your rain fly. Unexpected storms, passing showers, or even heavy doses of dew can all make for an uncomfortable experience if you aren't adequately prepared.

Bring water

Even though you're surrounded by water, chances are you'll need to pack a decent supply of your own, or invest in some water fil ters or purifying tablets before heading out. Sea water, because of its salt content, cannot be consumed. So unless you're absolutely sure that there's a fresh water source nearby, be sure to BYOW. If you're camping near a lake, river, or stream, you still need to be cautious. Unless you're at the source of a pristine, glacier-fed spring, you're going to need to purify any water before drinking it, regardless of how clean it appears to be. It's important to stay hydrated and in this case, it's definitely better to be safe than sorry.

Trash

Beaches are beautiful and your job, as a camper, is to help keep them that way. As with any campsite, you are responsible for your garbage and should be mindful of this when planning your trip. Cans and bottles are a hassle to transport and need to be brought back out so try to avoid using them in the first place. Consider packing some extra large freezer bags to use as trash receptacles—just remember that you need to take them with you at the end of your trip. Some parks provide you with garbage bags so find out beforehand whether the spot you're going to offers this service. Be sure to check ahead to find out if there are any restricted items you should just leave at home.

RV CAMPING

RV stands for Recreational Vehicle and RV campers embrace the liberty of traveling at their "own time" and are able to camp in different places while not sacrificing comfort that RVs offer. An RV is comparable to a small lodge but on wheels and normally comes complete with heater, oven, refrigerator, shower, stove, beds, toilet, and "12-volt" electrical power. According to many RVrs, they enjoy their "mini hotel" because they are always "packed and ready-to-go". Furthermore, they enjoy the cooking, bathing and sleeping convenience the vehicle offers while in a distant or remote campground. For individuals who have never experienced camping in an RV but are thinking of purchasing one, renting first would be a very sensible decision so you will see if the RV lifestyle suits you.

RV ownership is at a record high with **11.2 million households** owning an RV in 2021, up 62% over 6.9 million households in 2001 and 26% more than 8.9 million RV-owning households in 2011. This form of camping is gaining significant popularity across a wide variety of campers.

CAMPING BY THE SEASON

"Nature gives to every time and season some beauties
of its own; and from morning to night, as from the cradle
to the grave, it is but a succession of changes so gentle
and easy that we can scarcely mark their progress."
— Charles Dickens

WHAT IS THE BEST SEASON FOR YOU TO GO CAMPING?

Different camping seasons impart different lights and views. All seasons have their ups and downs. It's really about your preferences, tolerances and the experience you wish to enjoy. There is no wrong time to go camping.

Summer Camping

The summer is the most popular season for campers because the weather is dry and warm. Campsites are understandably more crowded during the summer. You need to plan ahead, make reservations and arrive early to find a good campground, especially during weekends. Also, the summer is when you will find the bugs out. So if you come, bring bug spray! You will need it. And the temperature is hot so you will need to monitor yourself to ensure you are getting enough water while you hike about in the heat.

Summer camping can be just as enjoyable as any other time of the year when you're prepared. In fact, summer camping opens up the option of swimming and other water sports.

Here are some reminders for summer camping:

1. Pack LOTS of Water
No matter the season, packing lots of water is a no-brainer. You'll need it to drink, cook, and clean. However, the possibility of dehydration is greater in the hotter summer months, especially when participating in activities like swimming where you may not even realize you are becoming dehydrated. Packing larger jugs to keep at the campsite and smaller bottles for daily excursions is also a good idea. In an emergency, electrolyte packets like these can be quickly mixed in water bottles for adults and kids.

2. Be Prepared for COLD Weather
Unless you're camping way up in the mountains, the summer months are typically going to be HOT. However, nighttime temperatures can dip low quickly. Make sure you're prepared with extra blankets and warm clothing including socks, coats, and hats. Body warmers can help to warm extremities quickly.

3. Be Prepared for Rain
Summer can bring about some torrential storms, and if you're tent camping, lightning and thunder would amount to a no-doubt-get-out situation. However, a little rain doesn't have to end your adventure. Pack extra tarps. They are affordable, easy to pack, and versatile. You could suspend one above

your tent for an additional layer of protection from the rain. Additionally, they can protect your camping gear and firewood from getting soaked. Bring extra trash bags to use as personal ponchos if rain strikes while you're away from camp.

4. Bring Swimwear

It is summer, and your campground is likely to have a pool, lake, or creek that you can cool off in. Be sure to follow campground rules and never swim in unknown or unmarked bodies of water. Bringing flotation devices and life vests is a must, especially if you are swimming in areas without lifeguards.

5. Remember the Sunscreen

It is easy, especially when camping in heavily wooded areas, to forget something as simple as sunscreen, but it is essential for your entire family's enjoyment. If you have ever had to soothe a sunburnt baby or have had to sit out a fun activity due to your own sunburn, you get it. Be safe and remember to reapply every few hours or after swimming. Wear a ballcap for added sun protection with the extra benefit of preventing ticks from getting in your hair.

6. Bring Insect Repellent

You'll find quite a bit more of these biting pests during the summer months almost anywhere you camp. Though we find spray repellents with DEET to be most effective, there are natural plant-based alternatives that will help some. If you'd rather not apply products directly to the skin, you can find a variety of citronella candles or coils or even electric bug zappers to control the bugs. Just be certain a bug zapper, which can be loud, won't annoy any neighboring campers.

7.   Pack a Fan or Two

Chances are, it will be hot during the daytime, and tents will warm up and retain heat well into the night. Using a fan to keep air moving inside the tent will keep the indoor air from feeling stagnant and mildewy. Additionally, you can use one of your extra tarps or a pop-up tent to make a shaded space and keep an extra cooler just for ice and cool towels for quick cool-down situations.

8.   Modify Your First-Aid Kit

Packing a first-aid kit is essential when camping with the family, however, you will want to modify it to support summer-specific ailment possibilities. Sunburn, bug bites, and encountering poisonous plants are at greater risk during the summer. So, make sure you have cooling gel, anti-itch cream, and calamine lotion in your standard first-aid kit. You may also want to consider anti-inflammatory painkillers to treat bug bites and burns.

9.   Bring Calorie-Dense Snacks

Like hydration levels, blood-sugar levels can drop quickly when you are out on an adventure. Bring plenty of calorie-dense, individually-wrapped, and non-perishable snacks for daily outings when you may not be able to get back to camp to eat right away. Items like beef jerky can satiate the hangry family member until you are able to sit down for a meal.

10. Keep Meals Simple

One of the best parts of camping is cooking around the campfire, but reserve this for nighttime only. Temperatures are cooler then, and you won't run the risk of overheating. Breakfast foods like cereal, yogurt, and fruit can get you started. Lunch meats and cheeses are easy to pack and do not require heating. You could also try self-heating meals designed for camping and other activities and do not require cooking. Do not forget the importance of storing your food in a locking cooler, especially in bear country. If possible, check with the campground or park ranger for their suggestions.

11. Choose Clothing Wisely

Moisture-wicking fabrics can help you stay cool and dry on hot summer days. This will be paramount where bathing facilities may not be readily available. Shirts and pants with sun protection are also good choices. Though wearing long pants may seem counterproductive to staying cool, a breathable pair will not only protect you from the sun but also bug bites and poisonous plants.

12. Set up a Cleaning Station

Sweat mixed with sunscreen, bug spray, and dirt can leave you feeling gross. No one wants to head to bed like that. Set up a cleaning station where you can at least wipe away some of the grime before turning in. A large, five-gallon jug of water with a spigot and a plastic tub makes an ideal wash station. Make sure you use biodegradable soap and dump your used water away from the camp to avoid making muddy puddles. Additionally, bring a few packs of baby wipes for quick clean-ups.

13. Contain the Kids

This really only applies to the very small ones who might like to wander away. If you have mobile tots, be sure to bring a playpen or other containment system. With so many things to explore at the campsite, it's just too tempting for the wee-ones to take off.

14. Plan for Downtime

Even if your chosen campground has more amenities than an amusement park, you can still expect some downtime. Personally, we cannot think of much worse than trying to cool off and relax with a cold beverage of choice while our children whine about how bored they are. Plan ahead and make up scavenger hunts for older kids or bring board games, cards, or even puzzles for younger kids.

15. Use the Sun

Summertime, typically, means lots of sun. Though it's essential to protect your family from it, you can still use it to power a range of devices. Solar-powered camping lights and lanterns can help you see around your site at night. Additionally, you can find solar-powered charging stations, wifi stations, fans, heaters, and even food freezers. Take advantage of the sunny days, but bring a stash of batteries just in case.

WINTER CAMPING

Winter camping is a wonderful way to get in touch with nature, build character and enjoy good times with your family and friends. These are some of the benefits of camping in cold weather and safety measures to keep you healthy and warm.

There are some people that find winter camping more satisfying compared to the summer months, because they say, winter camping requires a specific strength and courage that summer camping does not. If you love the challenge it brings, then consider "winter camping". You can enjoy sleeping in "mild weather" outside.

Likewise, it gives you added "self-confidence" realizing that you actually can endure the preparedness and ingenuity this kind of outdoor adventure requires.

Certainly, there are many advantages to camping during winter; no snakes, bugs, flies, bears, dust or mosquitoes, plus the winter wilderness view is breathtaking.

BENEFITS OF WINTER CAMPING

1. Deepen your appreciation for nature.
It's easy to love a spring day but winter can be more demanding. Whatever the hardships, enjoying fresh fallen snow and longer star-filled nights may convince you that the effort is worthwhile.

2. Learn to work as a team.
Everything will be harder when you're outdoors in cold weather. You'll need to pull together to get the tent up before it gets dark and make breakfast when the ground is frozen.

3. Experience solitude.
When the summer crowds are gone, you'll have a lot more space to yourself. Enjoy the silence and the chance to see more wildlife.

4. Persevere through obstacles.
Success in life often depends on being able to persist even when you run into complications. *The skills you learn while camping will help when you're pursuing other goals.*

5. Become patient with discomfort.
Much of the stress in life comes from our mind rather than from external conditions. You'll return home a little wiser when you see how you can make cold feet feel warmer by remaining calm.

6. Learn eco-friendly habits.
Many campers are becoming increasingly conscious of leaving as little behind as possible. You'll help build a more sustainable world as you focus on ways to reduce your footprint, including using alternatives to burning fuel.

You can go snowmobiling, snowshoeing, "cross-country skiing" and engage in many heartening challenges. Furthermore, campgrounds during winter will most likely be quiet, empty and normally cheap.

However, lack of preparation and readiness brings dangers. There are many hazards and dangers that one needs to be familiar with, like large quantities of snow falling from "overhead trees". But with good planning, you can enjoy the slower pace of winter camping.

Here are some reminders for winter camping:

1. Drink plenty of water to fight or avoid hypothermia because water effectively replaces all the moisture that was expelled from the body due to constant heavy breathing. Just drink water even when you feel you are not thirsty. The recommendation is one gallon of water a day.

2. At signs of an approaching storm, immediately put your rain gear on. Should you get wet, change right away to

warm and dry clothing, because moist clothes will quickly suck heat from your body.

3. Remember to pace yourself. Check the weather report and pay attention to local advisories. Play it safe with your own life and the lives of rescue personnel. You may be going into areas without a cell phone signal so ***ensure that someone knows where you're headed and when to expect you back.***

4. Do more tasks than you would normally, because movement will generate body heat.

Following tips 1-4 and wearing clothing layers, especially clothing that is polyurethane foam insulated will help you prevent frostbite. Trap body heat by dressing in layers, starting with long underwear. ***Half your body heat really can escape through your head*** so choose your hat carefully and wear it all the time.

Always listen and take notice of your body's reactions. When you start to shiver, immediately do something in order to make yourself warm before uncontrollable shaking and numbness sets in.

Take note that hypothermia occurs mostly in windy and wet weather with temperature ranging from "30-50 degrees F".

5. **Get the right gear. *Selecting the right equipment will make it easier to protect your wellbeing and have a good time.*** Check out winter tents that provide more coverage and stakes that are designed for snow. Chemical heat packs can keep your hands and feet toasty.

6. **Eat hearty.** You may need to eat more calories than usual because your body will be burning them up to fight the cold. A bedtime snack is especially good for raising your temperature a little. Focus on complex carbohydrates that are easy to carry around and simple to prepare

7. **Turn heaters off overnight.** Portable heaters can cause carbon monoxide poisoning if used improperly. Read the manufacturer's instructions and turn them off before you go to sleep.

If you've been putting your tent away as soon as the weather turns cold, you may want to give winter camping a chance. With some simple precautions, you can stay safe while you experience a new sense of peace and adventure.

FALL CAMPING

Fall camping is catching on among family campers. The beauty of nature during the fall season is indeed captivating.

With lesser crowds and no insects to bother you, fall camping can be the perfect option for you. However, during fall, some essential camping amenities such as showers and washrooms might not be offered. But, if you can settle on remote fall camping, pack your warm clothes then enjoy the "autumn months". Of all the months this season brings so much fullness of heart. Warm meals, hot fires and brisk evenings in the sleeping bag. Here are some items to consider when Fall Camping:

1. **Stay Occupied**
Whether it's a day hike with the family, rock climbing, or a rousing game of charades, having some sort of objective will

keep you warm and having fun, rather than focusing on the weather. Staying active throughout the day will not only help you sleep like a baby at night, it will also justify eating a big meal.

2. Bring Rain/Wind Coverage
Try setting your tent up in a protected zone and you'll notice a discernible difference in how long you sleep each night. Making sure to properly stake out your tent and rain fly will also help with both wind and, most importantly, drainage- prevent rain from soaking your whole situation.

3. Layering is Key
Layers of clothing in a mix of wool, fleece, and synthetic materials will help wick away sweat, and shed rain. Long underwear, a knit hat, gloves, insulator jacket, and a wind and water-resistant outer layer will go a long way to keeping you warm, dry, and comfortable this fall.

4. Eat like Kings
Eating a hearty, warm meal can make a huge impact on your physical and mental state. Not only can you excuse your gluttony after all your physical activity, but digging into a nice big meal will help fuel your body, replenish your muscles, and keep you warm through the long, cold night. Not only are one-pot meals delicious, they leave but one pot to clean.

5. Upgrade your sleep system
Waking up freezing cold at 3 a.m. is a terrible way to start the day. Adding a quilt or blanket to your kit and using a higher R-value mattress can make a big difference between time spent sleeping and time spent staring at the tent ceiling. Share body warmth with a buddy by zipping two sleeping bags together.

6. Fire it Up

Campfires are always an integral part of camping, and when there's a frost in the air they can make the difference between a 7 p.m. or 11 p.m. bedtime. When you get a good group around a campfire it's easy to forget how cold it is outside that orange glow. Be particularly careful this time of year around your management of fire breaks and camp fire management. Leaves are falling and dry this time of the year and so the forest becomes a tinderbox. Fire safety is your top priority during this time of year.

7. Alcoholic Beverages

While it's a myth that drinking alcohol warms the body—it actually does the opposite—it sure does warm the soul. Keep in mind that alcohol actually thins your blood, making your body temperature drop, so the more you drink, the colder you'll sleep.

SPRING CAMPING

Spring is the season of transition; snow is now melting away and it is time to go back outdoors and see nature after that cold and long winter.

So what is there to do during spring camping? Anglers are eager to go fishing because the "smallmouth bass" and the walleye are both spawning; ducks are now coming back and you can go hunting. Hike, swim, go canoeing, fishing, boating and do not forget to bring your paint brushes and camera as well because you will see more exciting sights. Likewise, you can set up a barbeque outside, of course far away from your tent and enjoy hearty grilled snacks and meals such as hotdogs, burgers, steaks, fish fresh from the river, vegetables and salads.

- **Be prepared for cool days.** Don't forget the fleece and jackets yet. Wind and cooler temps than you expected can be chilly, even if the sun is shining.

- **Layer your clothes.** It is easy to remove and add clothes as the temperature changes throughout the day.

- **Be prepared for cold nights.** Even if it is warm during the day, evening temperatures will drop. Be sure you have sleeping bags and blankets that can handle the lower temperatures.

- **Be prepared for spring showers.** Rain is common in the spring, so pack rain gear. Bring a rain jacket and consider bringing rain boots (for the kids especially) or an extra pair of shoes.

- **Be prepared for mud.** Along with the rain showers comes the mud! That's when those extra shoes or rain boots come in handy.

- **Put a mat at the entrance of your tent or camper.** It will help catch some of the mud and debris and keep your tent cleaner.

- **Be prepared for wind.** Stake your tent, even if it is free-standing and doesn't *have* to be staked. The same goes for a pop up canopy. It only takes one gust of wind to carry a pop up canopy to the neighboring campsite.

- **Be prepared for snow.** Snow in the spring? It is extremely rare in the south where I live, but other parts of the US do have snow in the spring. Check the forecast and bring the proper clothes and gear.

SPRING CAMPING ESSENTIALS

Check your camping gear. If you haven't used your camping gear all winter, be sure to check it out before you go. This will give you a chance to repair or replace anything that is broken or missing.

Pitch your tent at home. Look for any damage to your tent and make sure that no parts are missing. This will also air it out and get rid of any musty odors.

Never pack up a tent when it is wet. If your tent is wet because of rain or dew when you pack it up to leave, take the time to get it out at home and let it dry. It dries best by setting it up, but at least hang it out to dry. A wet tent in storage will get mildewed.

Don't forget enough sleeping bags or blankets. Remember, spring nights can be chilly, so bring sleeping bags or blankets for everyone. If you are backpacking or planning on backpacking in the future, you'll want a sleeping bag that packs small and weighs less than traditional sleeping bags.

Use a sleeping pad. A **sleeping pad** under your sleeping bag will provide another layer of protection between you and the cold ground at night, keeping you warmer. Plus it is more comfortable!

Know what you need for your camp kitchen. Did you get a new camp stove or grill? Make sure you have the correct fuel that it uses – unless it is a charcoal grill. You may want to give it a trial run at home to be sure it works properly.

Don't forget your lanterns and flashlights. Darkness comes a little earlier in spring. You will definitely want flashlights and maybe a camping lantern. For many the classic gas powered lantern with glass windows has been the go to for camping lighting. But it's large to carry, hard to hand and makes noise. The upside is that it puts out a beautiful light that seems to last forever. You may want to choose other types of lighting.

- Electric lanterns are battery powered and most use LED (light emitting diode) technology. These offer a long battery life, good light output, rugged, safe around kids and quiet. You will need to be mindful of charging and battery requirements.

- Gas burning lanterns usually run on liquid fuel, propane or butane. The primary advantage is light intensity. You can light up an entire campsite with the light output provided by one of these.

- Candle lanterns don't produce a lot of light but the light they do produce is natural, soft and pleasant. They make no noise and are good for close up tasks like writing. But again they do not produce a lot of light and they must be managed closely to avoid lighting your campsite on fire.

For car-camping excursions, size and weight generally are not concerns. For backpacking, however, they are. To flood a campsite or tent interior with light, candle lanterns were long the traditional choice. Yet bringing a lit candle inside a tent, even within a lantern's casing, is a risky practice. Small, compactable, new-generation LED lanterns make far better choices today. Or, an LED headlamp might also provide all the light backpackers need.

SPRING CAMPING PLANNING

Check for campground opening dates. Some campgrounds close for the winter, so check for their opening dates when planning your spring camping trip. This is true even for campgrounds that don't offer reservations. You don't want to arrive at the campground to find it closed.

Campgrounds are not as crowded in the spring. This is just one of the things I love about spring camping. It is a great way to avoid the crowds of summer.

Make reservations. Even though campgrounds are not usually as crowded in the spring, consider making reservations if you are going to a popular campground. And many campgrounds require a reservation.

Plan early. It is best to start planning your spring camping trips early – in the winter or even the fall if you want to get reservations at a popular campground.

Spring Break camping is the perfect vacation. Skip the typical spring break vacation at the beach motel and go camping instead. Find a beach campsite if you are determined to hit the shore during spring break.

Summer, Winter, Fall, and Spring offer many different and exciting challenges unique to every season. Remember, whatever the season, while you are camping, you are dealing and living with the wild. Learn and apply your "basic survival" knowledge when the situation calls for it; stay alert and be prepared always.

FIRST AID

"Safety doesn't happen by accident"
— Unknown

Be safe, don't leave home without it: a first aid kit. Camping requires a significant amount of time away from civilization and a lot of active time walking, trailing and enjoying all the glory of the outdoors.

However, wherever there is camp away from real-world conveniences, the possibility of needing some form of first aid – however little – is a necessity. The following are a few tips and advice to pack that vital first aid kit when out camping.

FIRST THING FIRST, TAKE LESSONS

Believe it or not, there are a lot of classes available that provide first aid lessons. There is a basic EMT or emergency medical technician course that one could take. However, for those who do not have much time, short lessons are available. The American Red Cross provides such courses. Check your local community. Basic first aid lessons are generally inexpensive yet valuable once learned. Once such knowledge is acquired the training allows you to provide immediate care to an individual who is injured or sick.

Children should also be given basic first aid information. When camping with children, it definitely would not hurt if they are introduced to the first aid kit. Show kids the items inside the first aid kit, its purpose and when the probable time it might be needed.

Older kids may also point out certain situations wherein they could get hurt and what action you should take when such a situation occurs. A child who knows or has a basic idea of first aid will panic less once an injury or a slight emergency situation occurs.

FIRST AID KIT: WHAT TO PACK AND HOW

To better understand your first aid kit, do not forget to bring in a manual. The American Red Cross provides a good one. Also, a small Swiss Army Knife is a very useful tool to have on a camping trip. An emergency blanket should be brought as well. Be aware that a blanket made of wool could get wet and after which may smell bad and take forever to dry. There are emergency blankets that are lightweight and are easily packed.

A razor blade is great for removing splinters. Another tool to bring on a camping trip is a magnifying glass. In addition to finding pesky slivers a magnifying glass can be effective for starting fires on a sunny day.

Another handy and useful item to bring is a mirror. Mirrors are useful especially when signaling for help.

A thermometer is another item that could be brought on a camping trip.

A cold pack can be included to prevent any exhaustion that is caused by heat. It could also be used to treat away burns, sprains, bruises, swelling, toothaches and headaches.

A water packet – the sterilized kind – usually containing about four ounces of water is an efficient and useful item used for water drinking and cleaning a wound. Fortunately, this item has a shelf life of five years.

For wounds, a medical tape should also be brought in. Also, try to pack in threads and a needle. Gloves, safety pin, scissors, eye dressing, band aid as well as a wrap bandage that is elastic.

For any injuries involving the shoulder or arms, a triangular bandage should also be brought along. Gauze pads (a good supply) should also be brought as well as a bandage that is large and compressed. A wrap gauze should also be available when camping, wipes that are antiseptic, a lip balm (to protect the lips from the sun), and Neosporin (for kids with small wounds).

Meanwhile, for adults, a pain reliever should also be available. For children, a non-aspirin tablet should be available. Decongestants are a good medicine to bring. Antihistamines are a great option for adults. For a hot camping trip, do not forget to pack in a salt tablet. All in all, camping is fun if you are prepared for all the activities and experiences the outdoors will bring. And to best prepare, understand the environment where you are camping. Make sure you understand where the nearest medical facility is and how far it is from your camp is the vehicle to get you there.

TENTS

An essential piece of equipment, your outdoor camping experience is largely dependent on the quality of your tent. Which is why there is a huge quantity to choose from. The first and simplest way to narrow your tent choices is to decide the tent dimension that you require. Tents are constructed to house a specific number of individuals. A solo backpacker will be looking for a tent that is much smaller than a family of campers that require a roomier tent. Almost all tents are labeled with description and their capacity which indicates how many individuals the tent can hold comfortably.

Unless you are intent on having a collection of tents in different capacities or sizes, it is wise that you establish the largest number of individuals you believe will sleep in the tent. For instance, if you normally backpack with a companion but this summer are going solo, then it is wise to purchase a "two-person" tent.

There are four tent components to keep in mind: namely the poles, tent body, rain fly and the tarp which is some kind of footprint or ground cloth to extend your tent's floor life. Apart from these basic components, here are some guidelines in choosing the best tent for you:

1. Consider your needs. Know your particular camping requirements, such as where do you mostly go camping, at what season and would you be backpacking? And how many people will you be camping with. The answers can give you a clear idea of what type of tent you will need.

2. Set your budget. When you allocate a budget before you go looking for a tent, most likely, you will not overspend.

3. Tent weight and size. How many individuals will be sleeping in the tent? The size of your tent will not really matter should you go "car camping"; however, if your intention is backpacking, then consider a "light-weight" tent.

4. Tent features. Today, there are tent manufacturers offering a lot of features for their tents. Mesh panels allow the breeze to go in your tent, while at the same time keep the mosquitoes and bugs out, "shock-corded" tent poles allow speedy setup, waterproof and flame resistant for safety, a rain fly for added rain protection, etc. Make certain you choose the tent that best caters to all your basic requirements.

5. Make certain that you select a durable fabric tent. It will cost you more money, however this is definitely an area worth it.

6. Select the proper tent color. Inspect how the color of the tent transmits light well into the interior. Certain colors generate a brighter interior, whereas others create a cave-like and dreary ambience.

7. Take note that light colors are best for summer camping since they tend to be cooler whereas dark colors are able to absorb solar energy so that they are great when camping in cold weather. (Section below on Tent Color)

8. Check the tent's coating. Remember that you must see a waterproof and shiny coating inside the floor and rain fly. If this is not visible or you can not feel this on the tent's fabric, then it is not thick enough to withstand heavy use.

9. Know that your tent needs when camping in the summer are very much different compared to camping in the snow. Almost all tents available on the market have weather ratings. Make sure that you purchase a tent specifically made for a particular weather condition or season that you will be out camping.

10. Tent manufacturers. Various tent manufacturers have their unique design and name. Some are identified to make inexpensive tents, while others are well recognized to make high quality but expensive tents. Popular tent makers are Coleman, Wenger, Eddie Bauer and Greatland Tents. Choose a tent manufacturer that has been trusted for years.

While in the forest or wilderness the wrong camping equipment may not kill you, but it can send you packing off to a motel and cause you to regret having planned a family campout. For that well-planned and enjoyable camping vacation, take your time when you purchase your tent. Remember, it will be your home for a few days. Having the right tent will keep you comfortable and warm especially on rainy and cold nights.

TENT COLOR

What is the best tent color? This seems like a simple question, so it should have a simple answer, right? Well, it actually isn't that easy a question to answer. Is there a straight general answer to this question, or is it situational? Maybe when camping tent color doesn't matter at all?

Generally speaking, the best tent colors are lighter colors like light blues, grays, and greens because they reduce summer heat. Natural green and brown colors are great for blending in while bright colors like yellow or orange make camp easier to spot in thick woods. For most people camping casually there really isn't much of a difference between various tent colors. However, if you are hunting you want neutral colors or colors that blend in. If you're hiking in isolated areas where rescue might be necessary you will want a bright color that is easier to spot.

The good news is that there is no wrong color choice, but if you want to smoothen your experience in certain outdoor conditions, the right color for your tent will go quite a long way. The color of the tent affects the amount of light that gets into the tent, the amount that gets blocked, as well as heat and temperature. It also affects how well the tent blends with the environment, ease of being spotted in an emergency, and the ability to attract critters. That said, **bright-colored tents** let in more light and reflect most sun rays, therefore, maintain moderate temperatures. They are also easy to spot in case of an emergency and are certainly picture-perfect.

On the flip side, they attract a lot of unwanted guests like bugs, insects, and even people. **Dull-colored tents**, on the other hand, absorb more heat in cold weather, and blend into the environment, thereby keeping unwanted guests away. They can, however, be hard to trace in an emergency and are known to attract mosquitoes.That said, there is no right or wrong answer when it comes to tent color. The right choice depends on the character of the environment one is camping in and personal preference.

Fundamentally, however, the best of both worlds is a bright-colored tent, paired with a dark-colored rain fly as the ultimate solution. Here's more on the color of your tent and why it is essential:

Things to Consider When Choosing a Tent Color

The best color for a tent is going to depend on a variety of factors, especially those related to where, why, and what potential dangerous conditions are at play when you go camping.

1. Blending in With the Camping Environment

Sure, that bright orange tent looks good for social media, but how advisable is it for the wild? Wild animals are quick to notice invasions in their natural environment, and any unearthly colors will catch their attention. Neutral colors are therefore non-intrusive, which in all honesty is only fair since you are the stranger in their home. In fact, some camping sites and natural environments do not allow tents unless they are neutral and easily blend with the environment. Moreover, blending in will camouflage your tent.

2. Environmental Conditions

Colors behave differently when exposed to sunlight. Bright colors let in more sunlight during the day and moonlight in the night. They also reflect more light, keeping away the heat. Think of light as pure energy that is stored in the form of heat to understand this.

With that in mind, choosing a dull color can mean unbearably hot conditions on hot days, but could also warm up a tent during freezing winter days. During summer, when everyone desires to keep their tent as cool as possible, bright-colored tents will do. In winter, go for dull-colored options. Here are color options from the one that absorbs the most heat to the one that absorbs the least: black, violet, indigo, blue, green, yellow, orange, red, and white.

3. Keeping Uninvited Guests Away

Camouflaging will keep the curiosity of visitors at bay. But this can depend a lot on location. There are some limited studies suggesting that mosquitoes tend to be attracted to darker colors, though there are questions surrounding this. Your blood type and the amount of salt in your blood/sweat probably has far more effect on mosquito attraction.

If you're camping on the beach or coast for the first time, it is worth noting that seagulls tend to like bright green, so maybe keep that tent at home and bring out the blue instead. But the big question: do brightly colored tents attract bears?

This is sort of a yes/no situation. The color itself doesn't necessarily attract a bear. Bears really aren't any more interested in red tents than blue tents or green tents or orange tents. But bears are very curious by nature. Since a brightly colored tent can be more easily seen from a distance, this could theoretically get the curiosity of a bear. In bear country the more important things to do are to take precautions like bear sacks or food canisters, making noise, and being aware of your surroundings.

4. Ease of Spotting

In the middle of nowhere, anything can happen. Animal attacks, health issues, getting lost and physical accidents are just but a few. A luminous tent will give you peace of mind, knowing that in such crises, you will be found easily.

Additionally, in case you get lost, after all, this is the wilderness, a bright colored tent will be easy to spot, but this only works if you get lost during the day.

5. Aesthetics

Wondering where your taste comes in? We didn't leave that out either! Vibrant colored tents will give fantastic images for your social channels! The contrast is welcomed amidst the natural environment. Aesthetics should, however, be the last consideration, and only in open camping areas that are generally free of any dangerous creatures.

A bright color might be great, but the disadvantages of one will outdo its advantages deep in the wild. With those factors in mind, you can look at the environment (or environments) you will be camping in to make a final decision.

Best Color Tent by Environment

With these five things, outdoor enthusiasts can choose the best color for their adventures. Let's delve deeper into the top color choices for tents for different camping activities. Based on the functional purposes, the best color for outdoor adventures include:

Heavily Forested Area: Dark-Colored Tents
Ideally, a bright colored tent will come in handy in case you get lost. But honestly speaking, would you leave your navigational skills to the color of your tent? Comparatively, a darker colored tent will bring more advantages.

First, it will store more heat since these are cold zones, camouflage against bugs and wild creatures, and blend well with the trees and undergrowth. Despite this, beware of hunting zones. A dark-colored tent increases the risk of being shot at, no wonder orange vests are worn in hunting zones. Game won't run away because you have an orange or luminous green tent. That said, hunting zones are an exception.

Beach Camping: Shades of Blue
Beaches and UV radiation go hand in hand, hence sunscreens. Beach camping is no exception. To protect the skin, a good color choice for your tent will help a great deal. Yellow shades offer the least protection, while dark shades of blue offer the best protection. They have an increased ability to block and absorb UV radiation.

Open Camping Sites with Lots of People: Buyer's Choice
In open camping sites with huge masses, any color will do. From pink to white and black, it all depends on personal preferences. Brighter colors will, however, stand out, while dull colors will be less conspicuous. If you're one to sleep for longer, choose colors that block the sun out, but remember that hot mornings will make your tent unbearable.

Therapeutic Camping Expedition — Bright Colors
When camping to let go of stress, depression, and weariness from day to day life, go bright. Colors can impact your mood.

Greys will make you sad, black, depressed, yellows will brighten up your day, and blue will restore good health.

Final Thoughts on Tent Color

Outdoor enthusiasts have higher chances of picking the right color for various camping adventures. When confusion sets in, don't fret, simply choose your favorite color, because, in the long run, each color will have both pros and cons. No matter the extent of research, number of visits to tent shops, and immense consulting, no single color will sort out all difficulties. If in doubt, going with a dark rain fly and a brightly colored tent gives you the best of both worlds so you can stick out, blend in, and just enjoy whatever camping environment you happen to be in.

BACKPACKS

"I was amazed that what I needed to survive could be carried on my back. And, most surprising of all, that I could carry it"
— Cheryl Strayed

"It's just a bag." That's what most inexperienced campers say. Unknown to them, the choice of bag is no trivial matter as any serious camper will testify. You will never appreciate how a good backpack can benefit your trek until you try going on a major one using an ill-fitting pack.

Take for example the experience of a trekker who went on a trip to the Appalachians in 1994. Instead of an exhilarating camp experience, he had to go home broken and bleeding from the weight of an ill-fitting pack damaging his hips. A decade later – with him a lot wiser and experienced – this hiker, accompanied by a better fitting pack, made 960 miles of terrain – a much greater experience than having your trip cut short due to terrible equipment.

Now you know how important a good pack is, here are a few tips to help you choose a good pack for the journey that lies ahead:

1. Know what you need – hikers and campers vary sharply in camping preferences, some are very minimalist in nature and take only the bare essentials. Others take a lot more equipment on their trips. The amount and type of equipment you bring will definitely shape the decision you make towards what backpack you will need.

2. You can then do some simple computation on your space needs. Most capable sales representatives can give you the amount of space their bags offer. When doing this try using the measurement for the amount of equipment you take for the longest trip you expect to go on.

3. Is it comfortable – this is probably the most important consideration when choosing a backpack. The goal of every good camping bag is to help campers carry the most amount of weight with the least amount of effort – and inconvenience for that matter.

Good packs distribute weight efficiently, allowing you maximum comfort when carrying the pack. To know how well a pack does this, you will have to test the pack itself.

Designs always vary and backpack companies are always heralding a 'new and improved' technology for campers to try out. The only way to really know if these new bags work is for you to try them out. Most camp stores will have sand weights to place in the pack so that you can test how the pack holds up to the weight. A rule of thumb to remember is that the shoulder straps should carry about 30% of the weight, while the hips – being a lot more stable should carry about 70% of the weight. When testing the pack, make sure the shoulder straps are not uncomfortable or restrictive. Try moving around in them to see how much mobility the backpack gives you.

Most packs also have a sternum strap. These straps help stabilize the backpack. Sternum straps should be positioned below the collarbone to ensure comfort and stability. The hip belts on the other hand should not constrict your breathing, nor should they be too thick that they reduce your mobility.

1. Choose your frame – there are two types of frames to choose from – internal and external. Internal frames are slimmer and hug your body closer, making them ideal for hard trails since they are so maneuverable and do not restrain mobility. They are a bit harder to load though. External framed backpacks are great for beginners on easy trails since they are easier to pack. However, they are a bit stiffer and may restrict mobility. It's the best type of backpack for children and beginners though.

2. Extras – when purchasing backpacks consider whether the pack is compatible with weather sheets to protect your pack against the elements. Also consider how attachments can be adapted for your pack. Most packs have rings and snap-on pieces that allow for accessories to integrate with your pack.

In the end, a good pack is almost synonymous with a great trek. Choosing a good pack will definitely enhance your camping experience tenfold. Choose carefully, since your backpack will probably be your most trusted companion on all of your camping trips.

SLEEPING BAGS

"A great many people, and more all the time, live their entire lives without ever once sleeping out under the stars."
— Alan S. Kesselheim

The hardest thing about going on camping trips is getting a good night's sleep. Being out in the woods on the trail will certainly expose you to nature's worst. While you shelter yourself against the elements with a good tent, only a proper sleeping bag will help give you a good night's rest to power you up for the next day of activities.

While finding a "be all and cure-all" sleeping bag is virtually impossible, it is, however, possible to find a bag that will keep you comfortable for most trips – if not all.

When choosing a sleeping bag, take careful note of your needs. You will have to cater your choice of sleeping bags to the trips you most often make. Also, careful knowledge of the available types of sleeping bags will help you make a good decision regarding a sleeping bag.

The greatest issue when choosing a sleeping bag is whether to purchase a down or synthetic fill sleeping bag. Nothing provides comfort and warmth like down, and down is generally recommended for most outdoor camping trips with the family. However, in the event that it rains and your down-filled sleeping bags get wet, it is going to take forever to get your sleeping bags dry. Synthetic fill bags, on the other hand, give good warmth and dry quickly if ever they get wet. They are a bit heavier in comparison, though.

Sleeping bags usually have a temperature rating guide that you can review prior to purchasing. If your needs revolve around general purpose camping trips, you will want to purchase a three-season sleeping bag. These bags generally have a temperature-comfort rating of 10 to 20 degrees Fahrenheit. If you are a more specialized camper – for instance if you like going camping on specific seasons – you will want to purchase a bag that caters to that season. If you like camping during the cooler seasons, go for sleeping bags that offer more warmth – and if you need a bag for warmer climes, go for breathable bags that keep you cool even during the hot seasons.

Most winter sleeping gear should be rated for minus 15 to 40 Fahrenheit, while summer sleeping bags should hold up to the 10 to 20 degree Fahrenheit rating.

Here are few things you should look for in a good sleeping bag

1. Material – Most sleeping bags will be made of nylon, or polyester. These are the best kinds of material for sleeping bags. If you are a serious backpacker, try to avoid cotton material – especially the printed ones. If you are taking kids along, you will probably have to concede this point.

   For added comfort while sleeping, look for bags that have a lining of taffeta or other non-cotton material. These materials, in comparison to plain nylon or even some cotton lining, are more comfortable, breathe better, and warm quicker.

2. Shape – The mummy shaped sleeping bag is pretty popular nowadays, however, some people find them constricting, especially those that want a lot of space to wiggle around in while sleeping. Mummy shaped bags tend to be snug and comfortable for some people, plus they warm quicker. Rectangular and semi-rectangular bags are great if you want a larger space to sleep in. Bags made for two (Double bags) are the best bet for couples who plan to sleep together. Another option is to choose rectangular bags designed for zipping together—the bags need to be the same model and brand. A few bags also can be zipped together if one person chooses a right-hand zip and the other a left-hand zip.

3. Accessories and zippers – Make sure the zippers are double-sided and allow for opening on both ends without any hassle. You may want to look out for zipper hooks as well, which prevent the bags from inadvertently opening up accidentally. Also look for insulated draft collars that help seal in the heat around the shoulders and around the neck. Plus, dark colored bags are advisable since they absorb more heat and are easier to dry out than their lighter colored counterparts.

4. Sleeping Pads play two very important roles for getting a solid night's sleep in the great outdoors: cushioning and insulation. While it might seem like having a comfortable surface to sleep on is a pad's most useful function, its ability to keep you warm throughout the night is often more important.

   Here's how to choose a sleeping pad for camping or backpacking:

- **Types of sleeping pads:** Learn about the three basic types of pads and how they perform: air, self-inflating and closed-cell foam.

- **Intended use:** Decide which activity your pad is for: backpacking, car camping, winter camping, etc.

- **Warmth (R-value):** A pad's ability to resist or restricts heat loss to the ground is measured as R-value—higher R-values are warmer.

- **Sleep system:** Being comfortable at a particular temperature depends on many other variables, including the temperature rating of your sleeping bag. Correctly pairing your pad and bag in your sleep system is key to staying warm.

- **Features:** Decide which other features are most important to you: weight, cushioning, size, inflation ease and more.

While all these tips come in handy, you may still want to test your sleep setup to see if it fits your lifestyle. Some stores will allow you to test their products before selling them to you. If this is the case, don't hesitate to jump into a bag to try it out. With a good sleeping bag, you can look forward to more comfortable nights on your camping trips.

WHAT TO WEAR

"Never underestimate the power of a good outfit on a bad day."
— Finja Brandenburg

Bad clothing decisions on your camping trip can spell doom for any 'happy family' camping trip. Just because we all enjoy typically comfortable weather where we live, we can afford to wear pretty much anything we want. However, when venturing into nature for camping trips and treks, everyday wear won't be enough to protect you or keep you comfortable. Nature isn't really known to take it easy on those that venture into its extremes.

So for an assuredly enjoyable camping trip, you will want to be fully clothed against the elements. Over the years advances in clothing technology have spawned a lot of camping wear designed to help keep the elements at bay on your camping trips. However, with the glut of clothing choices, it can get a little confusing to find out which clothing best fits your needs.

Here's a rundown of the stuff you can find off the rack at stores to keep you comfy during your expeditions and the technologies behind them. Knowing their characteristics will help you find out how these technologies can benefit your outdoor life.

THE MATERIALS

The most popular materials for camping wear include technologies that allow water to escape the material, but don't allow any water in. Ever since man started intentionally developing materials for the comfort of campers and trekkers alike, the biggest problem they had to face was how to somehow draw moisture away from the surface of the skin so that the camper did not have to wear wet soggy shirts that made for bad temperature control. The new clothing had to accomplish this while keeping moisture out – it had to have some waterproof properties.

In response to this need, developers have unveiled three breakthrough technologies in the field of outdoor and sports apparel – microporous laminates, microporous coatings, and monolithic membranes. All these materials somehow allow water vapor to escape while preventing moisture from settling on the skin. The monolithic technology is particularly interesting since it absorbs water vapor into itself while using body heat to dissipate the vapor. The harder you work, the more heat you make, and the more vapor is dissipated making for an interesting bit of technology.

You may want to check garments nowadays for this or similar technology. This technology helps keep you dry and comfortable, and makes maintaining a good temperature easier – especially in unforgiving cold climes.

NYLON OR POLYESTER

Nylon has typically been the more popular of the materials used for outdoor wear. This is because it is scratch resistant and can endure the wear and tear of most outdoor activities, plus it is light and breathable. However, polyester, not to be outdone, has steadily become an acceptable compliment or alternative to nylon since it keeps the wearer warmer and absorbs less water than nylon. Look for the new breed of materials – keep with nylon to be safe, the newer polyester kinds do well too.

STAYING WARM

One of the critical needs of people outdoors is apparel that will keep them warm in extreme weather. As mentioned above nylon or polyester coupled with the newer micropore technology does a good job at helping a person stay warm and comfy. However, in more abject frigid weather, you will need extra material to keep you warm.

The greatest issue when choosing camping wear is whether to purchase down or synthetic fill material. Nothing provides comfort and warmth like down, and down is generally recommended for most outdoor camping trips with the family. However, in the event that it rains and your down-filled clothes get wet, it is going to take forever to get them dry. Synthetic fill clothes, on the other hand, give good warmth and dries quickly if ever they get wet. They are a bit heavier in comparison, though.

Fleece is a good in-between solution for your garments. Contrary to intuition, fleece still keeps one warm even when it is damp. It also keeps moisture away from the skin, keeping one dry and comfortable. Plus they are squishy and comfortable to the touch. .

When looking for good camping wear, remember that the above mentioned technologies are very helpful in keeping you comfortable throughout camping trips. Look at each alternative and find out how their advantages fit in with your personal camping needs.

LAYERS

Your base layers are important because they manage moisture and keep a layer of warm air near your body. Choose a wicking fabric such as polyester or ultra-fine merino wool to keep your skin dry so you stay warm and comfortable. Wool can have a cozier feel than a slick synthetic fabric, a nice touch in colder temps.

Underwear: For backpacking trips, underwear is a matter of preference: Some men prefer boxer length, some women prefer the boy-short cut. Some women swear by wool undies, others only wear nylon-spandex mesh undies. Some backpackers prefer not to bother with underwear at all. If you do wear underwear, make sure they're airy and breathable, (which means not super tight) and are not cotton—once damp, cotton takes a long time to dry, which is uncomfortable and can cause chafing and yeast infections.

A general rule of thumb: Bring two to three pairs of underwear. Rinse out a pair as often as you feel it's warranted.

Bras: Choose a pullover sports bra without any clasps. Those metal or plastic parts can dig into your skin if they end up under your pack straps. Consider bringing an extra bra, or bring a super-lightweight camisole to wear while your bra is drying.

Tank top/camisole: A versatile piece, this lightweight top has many functions: adds to core warmth, makes a lighter alternative to a T-shirt and makes a good sleep top on warm nights. They may be made of silk, fine wool or synthetic fabrics.

Base layer top and bottoms: Also called long underwear, and available in different weights, these are a must for cool- or cold-weather backpacking. Choose from crew necks or zip-necks, which are a nice option for their ease of venting. Bottoms are multifunctional: You can hike in them under rain pants on rainy, chilly or windy days; they feel good to put on when you arrive in camp; and you can reserve a clean pair to sleep in.

Outer Layers

In general, bring one to two T-shirts, one long-sleeve shirt and one pair of lightweight yet durable synthetic pants. A pair of ultralight running shorts with a built-in brief can be a boon for hot weather: You can also swim in them and wear them while you wash and dry your pants.

T-shirt: Again, go with wool or synthetic. One tip is to bring two tees: one for hiking, and one to keep clean for sleeping in.

Long-sleeve shirt: Here's where locale comes in and where specific fabric benefits come into play. If you'll be hiking in the sun-drenched Southwest, for example, it's smart to bring a long-sleeve shirt rated UPF 50+ (many have an extendable collar for added neck protection). If you'll be trekking Northeastern forests, consider a long-sleeve shirt as well as long pants that contain an insect repellent to discourage ticks, mosquitoes, no-see-ums, black flies and more.

Convertible pants: Creek crossings and hot weather make convertible pants a good choice. Zip-off pants give you a real pair of shorts with nice gear pockets, but can be fussy to reattach; also, some find that the zipper can dig into their legs. Roll-up pants are a popular option, with button tabs above the ankle or near the knee. Cinch-pants also let you adjust the length.

Yoga pants/tights: These are a comfy choice for putting on at camp. While stretchy and easy to hike in, if your trail involves any rock scrambling or dense brush, think twice: They won't be as durable as nylon pants. (Tight clothing also does a poor job of protecting you from mosquitoes.)

Hiking skirt, dress or skort: Most are stretchy and skorts have a built-in liner. An insulated hiking skirt over yoga tights can be a great way to add warmth in cooler weather.

Fleece top: This is one of your most versatile pieces. On colder days, you can wear it while hiking and/or sleeping. On warmer nights when you don't need to wear it while sleeping, it serves as a soft pillow. Even if you've been hiking in a tee all day, a fleece feels good to pull on as the sun goes down. To save ounces, choose one with a quarter zip and no pockets.

Puffy insulated jacket or vest: Again, depending on the weather forecast, you may want a fairly substantial down jacket if it's going to be cold or snowy. If milder temps are on tap, bring a down vest, lighter-weight down jacket or synthetic insulated puffy. It's good to be prepared for any sudden downturn in temperature. Any of these should compress compactly.

Soft shell: A third option is a soft-shell jacket. Often these are water-resistant (not waterproof), may block wind, and may have a light fleecy lining for a bit of warmth. You still need to bring a solid rain jacket, though, for keeping dry in a storm, and soft shells are not very compressible.

Rain jacket and pants that are waterproof and breathable, which makes them fairly comfortable to backpack in. Remember: Keeping dry is key to avoiding hypothermia.

Also choose a jacket that's got pack-compatible pockets and an adjustable hood so you retain visibility as you hike. Pants with full-length side zippers can be the easiest to get on and off while leaving your boots on. Look for pants with an elastic or adjustable waist, and pockets, which are nice to have.

Must have accessories

Socks: Socks are one of the most important items you can bring backpacking. If possible, try out all kinds of socks and sock combinations well in advance of a long backpacking trip so you know what feels good with the boots or shoes you'll be wearing. A wool/synthetic blend with plenty of cushioning works best for a great many people, especially those wearing boots. Many people like to wear a pair of thin liner socks underneath a heavier pair. If you'll be hiking in trail runners, you may want a lighter-weight pair of socks.

Sock tip: When you stop for a lunch break during the day, take off your boots and socks and let your socks dry in the sun. Dip your feet in a stream or lake if there is one, and let them dry out too. Do the same at the end of the day in camp, so you go to bed with clean, happy feet in a clean pair of socks dedicated to sleep.

Hats: Bring two types: one for sun protection, one for warmth. If you're fighting sun in the desert, consider a wide-brimmed hat or a billed cap with a sun cape attached. Your warm hat can be a simple wool or synthetic cap, one you can also sleep in. A stocking cap doesn't take up much room in the bag and is a welcomed addition to a cold night in a tent.

Gloves for warmth: As long as the weather stays fairly mild, you can get by with a pair of stretch three-season gloves with a smooth exterior that resists light moisture and a fleecy interior that offers a little warmth.

Gloves for sun: Even our hands need UV protection, so wear sun-blocking gloves on desert hikes. These can be full-fingered or half-fingered and can be found in hiking or paddling departments. Look for a pair rated UPF 50+, or at least UPF 30.

Other accessories: A cotton bandana (finally, cotton gets its day) or a polyester neck gaiter are great to have for all kinds of reasons. Either can be worn on your head to keep hair out of your eyes, or around the neck for sun protection (or warmth, in the case of the neck gaiter).

KNIVES

It's like 10,000 spoons, when all you need is a knife.
— Alanis Morissette

A must have for your camping adventure is a good and reliable knife. A sturdy knife or multi-tool will help you prepare food, cut cord, make repairs, fashion a roasting stick—or even save your life in an emergency.

Finding the best camping knife is about more than just convenience, it's about wilderness safety. If you don't have a good blade on your belt, you're not prepared for long trips in the backcountry. You can find an affordable camping knife for under twenty dollars. Or if you're looking for some quality steel, the best camping knife will last you years of heavy use. However, it can be hard to choose the best camping knife that would suit your needs out of the hundreds of options on the market. Most people don't have time to do all the necessary research. There's a lot to learn about knives before you buy.

Knives and multi-tools come in a wide variety of styles, designs and materials. The knife or tool you choose will be based on your intended use and activities. The best option for ultralight backpacking may differ from what you need for car camping or everyday use.

TYPES OF KNIVES

Knives range from no-nonsense, fixed blades to compact pocket knives, and specialized knives for scenarios such as water rescue or woodcarving. Since no one knife will suit every task, some people carry multiple knives. However, with some careful consideration you can select a single knife that will handle most of your needs.

Pocket Knives

With folding blades, pocket knives don't take up much space and are ideal for hiking, backpacking and everyday tasks. They also keep the sharp edge protected inside the handle when not in use. However, smaller folding knives tend to lack the ergonomics and stability of fixed-blade knives, and a non-locking blade may accidentally fold down on your fingers while in use.

Fixed-Blade Knives

Fixed blades offer more strength, heft and ergonomic comfort than folding knives. They are easier to clean, but also weigh more, take up more space and require a sheath to carry safely.

KNIFE FEATURES

Locking Blade

A locking blade combines the stability of a fixed-blade knife and the convenience of a folding knife. The blade folds down for compact, protected carrying, but locks into place when you open it to keep the blade from accidentally folding down while in use.

One-Handed Opening

Some folding blades are designed to open quickly with one hand. A smooth folding mechanism and a stud, notch or cutout on the blade make it easy to push the knife open with your thumb. An ambidextrous knife can be opened easily with either hand.

Assisted Opening

When you start to open the blade, an assisted-opening mechanism engages and fully opens the knife. Assisted-opening knives feature a safety lock that disengages the mechanism when the knife is closed to prevent the blade from opening accidentally.

KNIFE BLADE MATERIALS

Ideally, a knife blade should resist corrosion, retain a sharp edge through sustained use and sharpen easily. However, there are trade-offs to consider: Harder steel holds a better edge and is less resistant to rust, but is also more difficult to sharpen. Softer steel may have higher corrosion resistance and is easier to sharpen, but usually doesn't hold an edge as well.

Stainless Steel

Most blades are made of **stainless steel,** an alloy that resists rust and corrosion. Three popular examples of stainless steel used for knife blades include:

- **420HC:** This affordable stainless steel resists corrosion, sharpens easily and features fair edge retention.

- **154CM:** Higher-grade stainless steel contains a higher amount of carbon for more hardness and good edge retention.

- **S30V:** Premium stainless steel contains a high amount of vanadium (a rust-resistant carbide that adds wear-resistance and toughness to a blade) for superior edge retention.

High-Carbon Steel

Some knives are made with non-stainless high-carbon steel. These blades feature outstanding hardness and edge retention, but are much more vulnerable to corrosion than stainless-steel blades.

KNIFE HANDLE MATERIALS

Often textured for improved grip and shaped for ergonomic comfort, knife handles are made of a wide variety of materials to suit your intended environment, aesthetic tastes and preferences for feel.

- **Wood handles** are beautiful and provide good grip, but are susceptible to water damage.

- **Plastic handles** are affordable and resist water damage, but can be slippery.

- **Rubber handles** offer great grip and water resistance, but can lack durability.

- **Stainless-steel and aluminum handles** are durable, but can feel cold and slippery in your hand

MULTI-TOOLS

Like a tiny toolbox in the palm of your hand, a compact and versatile multi-tool performs many more tasks than a traditional pocket knife. While their smaller size and reduced ergonomics make them less powerful than full-size tools, multi-tools are more than capable of handling many of the small repairs and projects you encounter in outdoor adventures and daily life.

Some multi-tools offer an activity-specific selection of implements.

Implements

Multi-tools are typically built around folding pliers as the centerpiece of their functional design. Common implements include one or more blades, standard and Phillips screwdrivers, scissors, wire cutter, saw, file, bottle opener and can opener. Other implements often found on multi-tools include a corkscrew, tweezers, toothpick, wire stripper, ruler and awl.

CAMP TOOLS

Sometimes when you're enjoying the outdoors, a knife or multi-tool won't handle all your tasks. Here are a few more camp tools you may find useful.

- **Axes and hatchets** are great for splitting kindling and pounding tent stakes.

- A lightweight **folding saw** makes it easy to cut firewood down to size.

- Ranging in size from small handheld trowels to larger folding models, a **shovel** comes in handy for digging a cat hole when nature calls or smoothing out the ground at a rocky tent site.

- A sturdy **machete** is a champ at clearing brush and for light chopping tasks.

CAMPFIRES

"The fire is the main comfort of the camp, whether in summer or winter and is about as ample at one season as at another. It is as well for cheerfulness as for warmth and dryness."
— Henry David Thoreau

One of the most memorable times you will have each camping trip will be building a good fire for your camping trip. Technological improvements to camping gear today makes traditional campfire building look like something a caveman would do, but knowing how to build a proper campfire can spell the difference between life and death in extreme circumstances.

There was a time not so long ago, when matches and gas torches were a novelty, building a proper campfire was essential to any outdoor activity. To stay warm on cold nights you had to have a fire going. The fire is where people cooked a warm dinner for everyone.

While the art of making campfires has been all but forgotten – partly because matches have begun to seem more convenient – campfire making as a skill is still relevant and essential to any camper's repertoire of tricks.

First of all, the secret to starting campfires is to start them quickly. You can only do this if you have a firm grasp of what is needed to start a fire – heat, oxygen, and fuel.

Oxygen, while around us, is not always readily available to the campfire, you may have to arrange the fuel in such a way that it has adequate air supply. You may also supplement this supply by blowing into a cinder, or fanning an already blossoming flame.

Heat is usually generated for campfires by friction. You will probably use an assortment of methods to generate this heat – rubbing two sticks together, using flint stones, and other techniques. However, this won't give you a glorious fan of flames if you don't have the right fuel.

Fuel is what keeps your fire burning, and finding the right type of fuel is integral to your efforts at building and maintaining a fire. Building a fire by applying the heat to the logs isn't going to work. You will need tinder. Tinder is easily combustible materials that will burn quickly and hopefully emit enough heat and gasses to start a fire with larger pieces of wood.

Ideal tinder includes dry sticks, bark, dry leaves, and twigs. Use this kindling to start the fire and to help maintain it. But remember that you can only successfully build a fire if the larger, harder to burn pieces of wood burn.

At times when the campsite is wet and tinder is hard to find, you need to look for dry tinder on the dry side of the tree. This is easily found: just find the area that is out of the wind and rain. Then:

- Find tiny, dry twigs and sticks. Ideally, they should snap crisply. Gather at least enough to fill your hat. Then double it.

- Peel off outer bark and remove the dry inner bark.

- Find bigger, dry sticks you can whittle down to fine tinder the size of a matchstick.

- Gather bigger pieces of firewood.

Some common designs of campfires include:

Teepee – Teepees are great for quick fires, and last long into the night. It makes use of a lot of tinder, so you will need a good bunch of it. The longer burning wood is placed, balanced against each other vertically around the tinder. This makes sure that the heat and the gasses of the tinder are generated in a way to help the larger pieces of wood to burn. It is the perfect fire for boiling water and general purpose campfires.

Pyramid – You build a 'pyramid' of logs by laying the logs horizontally on the ground together, then building another layer on top of the next gradually forming a pyramid. Although this type of campfire is a little hard to start up, the advantage of such is that it generates a lot of charcoal that will be useful in the future. It will burn well and is quite a stable fire.

Parallel – The parallel fire puts the tinder in between two logs. This is an efficient burning fire since the insides of the log burn too – having the fire and heat going in a good, snug place between two logs.

Star – This is the type of fire you usually see in those old Western movies. The logs are laid out like spokes of a wheel. Tinder is placed in the middle. The fire is easy to maintain, although you do have to push each 'spoke' of the wheel towards the middle as the fuel burns up.

There are other types of campfires, all with specific purposes. But as with any outdoor skill, creating and maintaining any of them takes a lot of practice to get right. Treat fire with respect as it has the power to save and to destroy. Remember to follow safety precautions after using a fire – douse the fire with water or bury the remains of a campfire with dust and dirt. Fires left unattended may cause serious property damage, so always take precautions that nothing that shouldn't burn gets burned.

FIRE SAFETY

Enjoying the pop and hiss of a glowing campfire—not to mention the light and warmth that the fire provides—is one of the most enjoyable parts of camping. But building campfires comes with responsibility. A campfire that is not properly built, maintained, and extinguished can quickly become a hazard to the people, animals, and land around it. In the United States, people start nearly nine out of 10 wildfires. It's important to understand how to safely and responsibly enjoy your campfire.

These are the top 10 must-know tips for campfire safety.

1. Know the rules
    Before you strike a match, make sure you know the fire regulations of the campground or wilderness area in which you are planning to build a fire. Fire rules change, and a campground that allowed campfires the last time you visited may have a temporary ban on them if the risk of

wildfires is high. Pay attention to posted signs and check the ranger's station for current campfire regulations.

2. Use the pit
Most campgrounds provide a fire pit or fire ring in which to build a campfire. If a pit is provided, this is the only place you should build a campfire. If you're in a remote area where campfires are allowed but a pit is not provided, dig a fire pit in an open area away from overhanging branches, power lines or other hazards that could catch on fire. Once the pit has been dug, circle the pit with rocks, ensuring there is a ten-foot area around the pit that is cleared of anything that could catch on fire.

3. Build a safe campfire
Once your pit is in place, build a safe campfire. Start the fire with dried leaves or grass that will easily catch fire. Next, add kindling, small twigs and sticks that are less than an inch in diameter. As the fire builds, add the largest pieces of wood to the fire. They will keep the fire burning for a longer period of time and provide heat. Keep in mind that your fire does not have to be roaring. A small fire surrounded by rocks will produce plenty of heat for both cooking and warmth.

4. Mind the match
Start your campfire with a match and then make sure it is completely extinguished before disposing of it. Pour water over the match or throw it directly into the fire to burn. Never use lighter fluid, gas, kerosene, or other flammable liquids to start a fire.

5. Use local firewood

Though it may not be apparent to the naked eye, tree-killing insects and diseases can live on firewood. If you're going camping six hours down the road and decide to bring firewood from home you could, without knowing it, transport insects and diseases and inadvertently introduce them into the forests where they weren't found before. That's why it's so important to use local firewood. Local is defined as the closest convenient source of firewood that you can find. If possible, pick up firewood from the campground camp store or a nearby location.

6. Keep water handy

Don't start a campfire without having a bucket of water and a shovel nearby. The water can be used to douse any runaway flames and the shovel can be used to throw sand or dirt on any flames that jump the perimeter of your fire ring. It's also smart practice to keep a few feet of ground outside of your fire ring watered down, so if a stray ember or flame jumps outside of your fire pit, it won't gain any traction.

7. Pay attention to the wind

A strong breeze can spread your fire in an instant. To make sure a sudden gust of wind doesn't turn your campfire into a wildfire, keep anything flammable, including unused firewood, upwind and at least 15 feet away from the fire. The 15-foot rule also goes for your tent and clothing hung to dry.

8. Be careful with kids and pets

It's not just the risk of forest fires that you need to be mindful of while camping. Campfires are the leading cause of children's camping injuries in the United States. Teach your kids about the danger of fire and don't allow children or pets around the campfire unless they are on an adult's lap. Teach kids how to stop, drop, and roll in the event that their clothes catch on fire.

9. Never leave a campfire unattended
   A campfire should not be left alone, even for one minute. A small breeze can spread fire quickly, so there should be at least one set of eyes monitoring the fire at all times. Even if you're leaving the fire for a short period of time to take a quick hike, the fire should be completely extinguished. You'll be able to restart it once you return.

10. Put the fire out properly—every time
    When you are done with your campfire make sure it is extinguished properly. Dump water on the fire, stir the ashes with a shovel, then dump more water on the fire. The campfire should be cold before you leave it unattended. If it is too hot to touch, then it is too hot to leave. Large logs will be more difficult to extinguish than smaller logs so make sure they are also soaked with water. Move the stones around the campfire to check for hidden burning embers underneath. And never bury coals from the fire—they can smolder and start to burn again.

ANIMALS

"Animals don't hate, and we're supposed to be better than animals."
— Elvis Presley

The fire is important for more than the essential task of keeping you warm. Animals like feral dogs, wolves, coyotes, skunks, squirrels, and rats will avoid the fire. Generally speaking, nocturnal species will find the light of the campfire to be uncomfortable since their eyes are set up to see in low light situations, and looking into the fire can cause them pain or hamper their vision. Insects are also repelled by campfires, but it's not the fire or the light that does the repelling, the smoke does. Unfortunately, depending on the species of bugs present in your campsite you may need to create a lot more smoke or sit closer to the fire to experience any tangible benefit.

WILD ANIMALS A CAMPFIRE WILL NOT REPEL

Bears. Everybody is concerned about encountering a bear when they are out camping and need to know whether or not their campfire will keep them safe from them.

Bears are not repelled by a simple campfire regardless of species and will happily wander into your campsite. The good news is that most bears are not aggressive and are either simply curious or scavenging for an easy meal amongst your food stores. Raccoons are one of nature's most fearless scavengers and are unlikely to be repelled by a simple campfire. They tend to live in and around humans and live off of our garbage and food wastes so they are comfortable near fire and light despite being nocturnal.

Packs of dogs, wolves, or coyotes will overcome any fear that they might have had while solitary but luckily these animals will still tend to avoid humans unless they are starving.

In rare cases, a campfire may also attract reptiles like lizards and snakes looking to warm up. Although they are more likely to hide in shoes or sleeping bags for an unwelcome surprise.

Animals with rabies or that feel desperate and cornered are likely to buck conventional wisdom about their species due to their altered state of mind. Any animal with rabies will be willing to aggressively charge people at a campfire and a cornered animal will approach a fire.

So What Does Repel Them?

There are a couple of easy methods that will repel healthy animals that would not be dissuaded by your campfire.

1. **Make your presence known** – the cheapest and easiest way to secure your campsite from being visited by unwanted wildlife is to be loud and make noise. Most animals are afraid of humans, so if you are a loud confident human they will avoid the area. Belt out some off-key songs at camp or hold a simple conversation and wildlife will generally steer clear. If you need to sleep or don't want to talk the whole time, play a radio to simulate human voices and conversation.

2. **Use scents to your advantage** – I don't mean marking your territory like an animal would. The scents of urine and excrement actually *attract bears*. There are various liquid and solid animal repellents you can purchase, but if you want to keep it cheap and simple just use some fabric softener sheets. Place these sheets strategically around your campsite and make sure they don't blow away and your area instantly becomes less appealing since animals are very sensitive to these scents.

WHAT ATTRACTS WILD ANIMALS?

Animals are always using their noses to further their main agenda which is finding food. Sustenance is the main goal of any animal and this extends to staking out territory and investigating the marking of any animals including humans.

There are some common actions that humans tend to do that attract the attention of wildlife in camping or hiking situations.

1. **Cooking** – nothing gets the attention of animals more than the scent of cooking food. During the cooking process, a lot of scents are put out that attract hungry animals. If it is possible to cook in an area some distance from your camp you reduce your chances of an unwanted animal encounter.

2. **Food-related trash** – improperly disposing of food-related trash is a sure way to end up with your camp being raided by animals. It is important to dispose of all trash that is food-related or has food scent or scents that are similar to food in a durable odor-proof bag.

3. **Urine and excrement** – bigger animals like bears and mountain lions are attracted to the scent of urine and excrement. In large predator country, you need to be cautious and be 100 yards from camp before taking care of your bathroom needs.

Executing good practices relating to these issues will decrease your likelihood of unintendedly running into wildlife.

HOW TO AVOID CAMPING NEAR ANIMALS

You can save yourself from potential animal trouble if your campsite is appropriately placed. Some things to consider below when choosing your campsite below.

1. **Choose flat open ground** – flat open ground improves wind-flow and will alleviate insect-related issues.

2. **Minimal grass** – low grass or bare ground is a better choice when possible because of snakes and rodents that like to lurk in these areas.

3. **Fallen trees and deadfall** – fallen trees and deadfall often house insects, snakes, rodents, and other wildlife like raccoons.

4. **Trails and water sources** – animals tend to use the same trails and need water just like humans do. Avoiding these high traffic areas by being 50 yards away will reduce your chances of an encounter.

5. **Animal sign & droppings** – if you see scratched up trees or large droppings you should pick a different campsite immediately because it is possible that a bear or mountain lion has marked its territory and you want to avoid them at all costs.

6. **Talk to the ranger** – if you are camping in a state or national park you can talk to them about what areas have more or less animal activity and where sightings have happened. Their advice is invaluable since they are wildlife experts in the local area.

Following these simple rules, you can make your camping experience more pleasant.

ADDITIONAL PREVENTATIVE TIPS

Wild animals are naturally curious and will investigate new and foreign smells. This includes common items like toothpaste, deodorant, dish soap, and shampoo. Use these in the morning to increase the chances of the smell dissipating by nightfall.

Here are 6 more tips to lessen your exposure to an encounter with a wild animal:

1. Change into clean clothes prior to sleeping to further reduce the chances of cooking odors or other interesting scents being investigated in the night. Clean yourself and change around 50 yards from your campsite when possible.

2. Inspect your tent to ensure that there are no rips or tears in your tent and that all of the zippers are in working order.

Make sure all the zippers are closed before leaving your tent. Animals inspecting your campsite is one matter, finding them in your sleeping area is much more dangerous.

3. Shiny objects like keys, cutlery, and aluminum foil are attractive to many creatures, especially raccoons. To avoid contact with them just cover these items up before going to sleep.

4. Thoroughly wash down any cooking equipment and dispose of food scraps in appropriate areas. Waste-water from these activities should also be disposed of 50 yards from your camp.

5. Never eat inside your tent. Food odors being trapped inside your tent can attract animals and give them a reason to force their way inside.

6. Hang your sealed cooler and all of your supplies high in a tree in an odor-proof bag high off the ground, preferably over 10 ft off of the ground. Other options include a bear canister and storing your food in your car. However, it is important to realize that food stored in your car is only safe from smaller scavengers. Bears have been known to open and break into cars to investigate food smells.

WHAT TO DO IF A WILD ANIMAL SHOWS UP

Even if you do everything in your power to avoid it, it is still possible that wild animals could show up. If it happens, stay calm and don't panic. And use some of the tips below to increase your safety.

1. **Make loud noises** – clapping and whistling and bright flashing lights all scare away the majority of animals. Bears will also dislike these actions but you need to make sure that it is not done in a threatening or combative manner from a safe distance.

2. **Do not stare** – any direct eye contact with a predator is considered a sign of aggression so unless you are looking to be in an animal attack situation avoid doing this. Larger aggressive predators will attack if they feel challenged.

3. **Back away slowly** – backing away slowly will remove you from the situation in the safest possible way. Turning your back or even worse running from an animal may trigger an instinctive response to chase and hunt you as prey.

Following these simple guidelines could help keep you safe in an animal encounter. To be extra safe, try to read about local wildlife you are likely to encounter before camping or hiking and talk to a local park ranger to be as prepared as possible.

Will coffee grounds attract bears? Coffee is very attractive to bears, but not for drinking. Coffee grounds are very aromatic and since bears have such a strong sense of smell it is like catnip to them.

What smells will deter bears? Strong pine-based smells in cleaners are disliked by bears and tend to keep them away.

FINAL THOUGHTS

Campfires repel a wide variety of wildlife but not all types of wildlife. A campfire will not repel everything and it is important to take a broader view of your actions in the wild to repel or avoid animals.

Be aware of the situations you are creating and you can help to control the likelihood of encountering wildlife and the safety of yourself, your friends, and your family in the case of a wildlife encounter.

CAMPING FOOD

"Camping and eating food outdoors makes it taste infinitely better than the same meal prepared and consumed indoors."
— Fennel Hudson

When camping, it helps to think and carry light. However, no matter how pretty the image is of a campfire with eggs and tasty bacon sizzling in the background, plus hot coffee, reality bites. And reality is heavy.

In order to make this food camping image real someone has to carry all the cooking equipment needed, such as a cast iron pan, a cooler, as well as ice to keep food fresh, etc. The usual options therefore are frozen and dried meals which basically cost more, and have no taste at all. Plus they are heavy on preservatives and artificial flavors. Believe it or not, there are a lot better options out there at the grocery store nearest you which provides healthier, if not a lot tastier food options. And they are not just instant noodles.

The following are tips to choose the camping food that is right for you. Never eat inside your tent. Food odors being trapped inside your tent can attract animals and give them a reason to force their way inside.

WEIGH IN, WEIGH OUT

Camping requires a lot of energy walking and traversing trails and trees. So any stuff carried during this time must – as much as possible – be light in weight or at least tolerably heavy. This is because besides food, clothes also need to be packed, a sleeping bag, a system for purifying water, a mattress, and so on.

The cooking system used most during camping trips are stoves that involve micro cooking. This is composed of a burner primarily used to boil water. Usually any nourishment a camper would consume is food that is the dehydrated kind. Cereal like Cheerios is a good option. There are also foods that are the dehydrated kind. Also, there are packaged cereals that all you need to add is hot water so you can enjoy a warm meal. Oatmeal is one of them, also cream of wheat. It is best that these types of meals be placed in a bag, preferably a Ziploc bag so you can appropriately portion the quantity you would be taking and eating. Better this than bringing an entire package of oatmeal. Dried fruits, like raisins are also a better and healthy option. Cranberries that are dried are another, as well as blueberries. Another good thing with this type of camping food is that there is less trash left behind.

For drinks, good old powdered orange juice like Tang is readily accessible and easy to carry as well. Coffee could also be brought on a camping trip, the kind that could be made instantly and not brewed.

During camping, compared to bread, crackers are a better option because they stales a lot less and fill the stomach too. Plus they are light and handy. However, if you want cheese with your crackers, choose those that do not need to be refrigerated. There are available ones in the grocery. Or if you want to be tastily creative, there is always easily-packed pepperoni and salami.

Peanut butter can also be placed in portable tubes. Chocolate is another great option that can easily be packed and is extremely tasty and emotionally filling especially during that difficult climb to the top. However, if you prefer to experience a little of the luxury in the real world to your camping climb, – and do not mind carrying some heavy stuff – pack in a can of liver pate', chicken chunks, ham, or tuna.

Relax though, if you are having difficulty sacrificing your wants, try to think that your camping climb is not forever. You will eventually be coming back to the world where all the modern conveniences are there for you.

PREPARE, PREPARE AND PREPARE

Prior to camping, make sure that you know just how many days or weeks you will be out. This helps you prepare the meals that you need to take during your trip. To get the most nourishment without feeling too heavy after having eaten during camping, calculate the quantity of snacks you could take in. Usually carbohydrate rich foods do not have a lot of moisture and so are a good choice.

Also, to avoid a monotony of the same meals during camping, it is best that you schedule or designate different types of food at each meal. Dried fruit for breakfast and oatmeal for lunch are good choices. Cookies in between are not bad either.

All in all, camp food is just like regular food minus the usual amenities. It could taste good and be healthy too if you know where to look.

COOKING AND PREP

Use this as a planning guideline. The list below is neither exhaustive nor needed for all camp cooking. There is more on this list than you should bring with you to any one outing. Only bring what you need. Having too many supplies will weigh you down and make the hike to and from camp more strenuous. Plan out your meals and only bring the items needed for those meals. Likewise, you should have a backup plan for what to do if the weather doesn't cooperate. If you only bring raw meat and it's too rainy to build a fire, better have a propane stove and perhaps a tarp to shield it, or at least some no-cook snacks so that you don't go hungry.

- Grill rack
- Griddle
- Dutch oven and lid lifter
- Charcoal
- Firewood, sourced near the campsite
- Saw/axe
- Aluminum foil
- Portable coffee/tea maker
- Mixing bowls
- Measuring spoons
- Measuring cup(s)
- Marshmallows/hot-dog-roasting forks
- Rolling ice cream maker
- Hand-crank blender
- Camp table(s) or kitchen organizer unit

Setting the Camp Table

When it comes to serving meals, paper plates and plastic forks and spoons are tempting, but you can save space and help the environment by choosing lightweight, reusable items instead, like stacking cups, and aluminum utensils.

- Plates/bowls (at least 1 per person)
- Mugs/cups (at least 1 per person)
- Eating utensils (forks, knives, spoons)
- Napkins
- Water bottles
- Tablecloth (and clips)
- Lantern/lighting

Camp Kitchen Storage

Containers are important to keep your food safe for consumption.

- Cooler(s)
- Ice or ice substitutes
- Bear- and/or rodent-resistant food containers
- Egg holder(s)
- Small food containers (for leftovers)
- Resealable bags
- Large bins or bags (to transport and store kitchen gear)

If you're car camping or just going on a day trip, you'll have the luxury of a cooler, but it's not quite as capacious as you might wish, especially if you load it up with beverages. So, for longer trips, you should bring a separate cooler just for drinks. Speaking of, the old trick of freezing water bottles to use as ice packs (and later, to drink) is still a good one, although plastic bottles aren't exactly environmental all-stars. You can freeze lots of other things too, including meats and precooked rice in resealable plastic bags, which will help them last longer and contribute to the cooler's chill factor.

Camp Kitchen Cleanup

- Camp sink or wash bin(s)
- Large refillable water jug
- Biodegradable soap
- Pot scrubber/sponge(s)
- Trash/recycling bags
- Quick-dry towels
- Paper towels
- Dish-drying rack

See Appendix for Camping Recipes

CAMPING ACTIVITIES

You are only limited by your imagination. Always, there really is something fun to do if you just put your mind to thinking up ways to do it. The following may be helpful suggestions to do just that. Believe it or not, these tips do not require expensive devices, batteries or equipment. All one needs is an open mind and a free-wheeling attitude.

CREATE INTERESTING STORIES

Telling stories is the age-old device used by our ancestors - and even us - to battle away boredom. What did you think was the purpose of all those cave drawings? Story-telling is an ingenious way to keep kids and our minds occupied. An idle mind is a nest of anxiousness and tantrums. Keeping their minds creatively occupied through stories will get their brain cells processing. Plus, the best thing about this activity is it is free and could be done anytime and anywhere.

How to get started? Simply start with a single line. This line should set up or at least build up the image of where the story could lead to. For example, you may begin with "Once upon a time," or with "I saw a green marmalade monster once." From there, abruptly stop and let others add their own detail to the story. However, it is best that you also set up specific rules. You may advise that there should be no detail that would scare "your little brother," just good old clean and entertaining fun.

WATCH THOSE CLOUDS PASS

Relax and unwind. This is one way to unreel and be less uptight about anything. Chilling out has never felt this good. Spread some towels on the grass or a blanket that is old and not that regularly used. Lie on your back and observe the variety of clouds that pass by. You may see an elephant, a rabbit or a dog. Or you could count the number of clouds that pass. This is a relaxing activity that is also just as fun. Try it out.

BUBBLES, BUBBLES, BUBBLES

When outdoors, do not forget to bring your bubble maker device or toy and let everyone, especially kids, bubble their way to fun. This is an effective way to run around and laugh as bubbles pop and float around.

BOARD GAMES, DICE AND PLAY

In case you get rained on, do not fret. If you have brought your trusty old dice and any easy-to-carry board game with you, playing will be just as easy as one to three and it's fun too. The game Yahtzee is one example.

Card games are also easy and convenient games to bring. It fits one's pocket easily and can bring loads of entertainment and games. Even magic tricks, if you know a few ones using cards.

WRITE YOUR WAY OUT OF BOREDOM

Try bringing a journal and write your heart out. This could include a log of the activities that you have done all through the camping trip. They may be fun and educational later on.

STUDY UP

When in a new place, it might help if you study the area's history. This could be a good way to tell kids the background of the area where you are camping. It may also be a nice story to tell around campfires.

SING SOME SONGS

Really! Do not think of it as cheesy - it may be an effective boredom buster. Songs around the campfire is a good activity to keep everyone entertained. Make up a song. Or play a game by letting others guess the song you are humming. Use nature's instruments. Twigs may be used as drum sticks. Dance also. It does not cost a thing. It may also be a form of good exercise.

All in all, the limits of activities rest on how much you want your mind to explore. The sky's the limit may also mean, your mind is its own limit. Do not be afraid to try something everyone would enjoy and have fun doing. Be creative. You may also bring toys such as balls. Frisbees are also a fun thing to play with especially when camping in the wild outdoors. Just remember to always have fun.

PRACTICE MEDITATION AND AFFIRMATIONS

See some examples of Affirmations in the back of this book. Make them your own or let them inspire you to create. Being outdoors and thinking positively is a skill that will follow you wherever you go.

See Appendix for a few examples of affirmations.

KIDS AND DOGS

"Teaching children about the natural world should be seen
as one of the most important events in their lives."
—Thomas Berry

N o doubt about it, camping trips are fun. A vacation in the
wild outdoors, fresh air, roughing it can be such a fun
break from the hectic routine of city life. However, a lot of
people think they cannot enjoy or even survive a camping
trip because of kids. Children can indeed add enjoyment to
anybody's life, but to be honest, it is really hard to bring kids
along on a camping trip. Imagine having no television or com-
puters to keep them busy (and quiet). For the average parent,
that could spell disaster. But you should not despair; there are
many activities in the outdoors that can keep kids entertained
during a camping trip. Here are ten of them.

Get wet and go splashing. More likely, you would be able
to find a nice swimming spot. Whether a big lake or a small
brook, you are bound to locate a nice body of water to splash
around and have wet fun. Swimming amidst nature can be so
much more enjoyable than swimming in a man-made pool.
Just be sure that the swimming hole you find is safe for people,
normally camping parks would tell you which ones are good

for dips and which ones are not. Also, be careful about diving and never leave your kids swimming alone.

Bike together. Most camping sites have great bike trails. Riding bicycles is very fun when the view is great. It is faster and cooler than just traveling on foot. Make sure to bring a map and plan your trip so that you would not easily get lost. Do not ride too fast, or you might leave each other behind, anyway, you would not be able to enjoy the scenery if you speed.

Watch for birds and animals. Most camping sites and forest parks have primers and leaflets about the various animals thriving in their area. You may also bring books about wild animals and see if you could spot them. Try having a contest – the one who spots most kinds of animals wins. See the different animals that come out during the night and compare them to those that come out during the day. Just keep your children a safe distance away so that they will not disturb the animals.

Play games in the outdoors. It may be the classic sac race, tug-o-war, or just plain tag. Nothing beats the time-tested games when done in the woods. Just be sure to play games in a clear area to avoid accidents. Also, avoid creating so much noise so that you disturb the wildlife.

Organize a scavenger hunt. Kids love to go on quests and adventures. Scavenger hunts can be a great alternative to the role playing games kids play these days, not to mention that it is more physical, allowing your kids to exercise rather than just sit in front of the computer screen all day. Just warn your kids about the many prickly plants that could be lurking in the woods, such as poison ivy, oak and sumac.

Learn how to read maps and compasses. The great outdoors is a nice way to teach your children about navigation. Take out your map and compass while exploring the forest. Show your kids where you are on the map and show them where you are heading. This can also be done in conjunction with the scavenger hunt.

Light a campfire. Perhaps this is among the most awaited activities during camping. This can be the best way to end the day. Gather around the campfire to sing songs and tell stories (scary ones if you would like). Roast marshmallows and hotdogs. Play riddles and other word games.

Watch the stars. This is another night activity that can be both fun and educational. You may just simply lie on the ground and appreciate the free light show in the sky, or you may bring out a star chart and look for famous constellations and other heavenly bodies. Look for shooting stars and make your wish.

Bathe in the rain. The weather can be unpredictable in many places, you cannot expect to have clear and sunny skies all the time. But do not pout if the rain does pour. You can have fun playing in the rain and enjoy mother earth's natural shower. Just be careful not to go out when there is thunder and lightning.

Just relax and simply enjoy the moment. You are in the outdoors for only a few times a year (or even in a lifetime). Enjoy what nature has to offer. Avoid bringing any electronic gadget and simply bask in the quiet of the forest. This is the time to bond and enjoy each other's company.

There are hundreds of activities to do outdoors,but these ten are just a fraction of the many activities you can do with your kids on a camping trip. The point of it all is to enjoy spending time together as a family.

THE DOG

Camping is definitely a great way to spend one's vacation. The great outdoors is indeed a good venue to take time off from the hustling and bustling city with the fresh air and nice view that is a welcome replacement to your daily dose of smog and dust. However, many people are hesitant about taking camping trips, especially those who have pets. While pet hotels are now widely available, a lot of dog owners could not bear to be separated from their beloved canines even for just a few days.

One great idea to do is bring Fido along on the camping trip. Of course there are advantages as well as disadvantages with bringing your pet dog camping, it is therefore important to weigh the pros and cons carefully before deciding to take Fido along on your trip.

THE PROS OF TAKING YOUR PET DOG CAMPING

Bringing your dog camping can be very exciting for both you and your canine friend. The outdoors can be very stimulating for an animal that has spent much of its time in a yard or a secluded doghouse. Your dog would greatly be excited to see, smell, and hear new things. The fresh air of the woods can be very advantageous to your dog's health. The camping site can also be a great venue for the dog to exercise since you are most likely going to take a lot of walks in the forest.

Bringing your dog along can also free you of worries and the anxiety of leaving him or her behind. This gives you peace of mind during a time when you are supposed to be relaxing. While pet hotels have been really made to be safe for you pets, seeing your pet all the time is usually the best way to make sure they are safe and are being treated the way you want them to be.

When you bring your dog along, you can also do a lot of activities. You can take your dog on hunts for bugs and other small animals. You can play catch and fetch. Dogs can be great company for long walks. They can also help guard you from dangerous animals and nosy campers. Dogs are great protectors in the wild. A dog can even help you find your way back to your campsite in case you get lost.

THE CONS OF TAKING YOUR PET DOG CAMPING

Taking your dog camping can indeed be fun, but it can also be a hassle. Dogs can get overly excited in the outdoors. They can get rowdy and misbehave because of the new sights, sounds and smells that agitate them. They may also be frightened by the wild animals they might encounter in the woods. Being introduced to a large space might also exhaust your dog, especially if it is old.

Bringing your dog along may also give you extra things to worry about. Dogs may get lost in the woods and it would really be stressful on your part if they do. You might constantly need to check on your dog, giving you extra tasks during a time when you are supposed to be relaxing. Your dog can also be extra noisy especially at night, disturbing your sleep and the quiet moments. Dogs may easily get into accidents outdoors as there are many hidden dangers that lurk in the forest. They might run into cliffs or get entangled in bushes. They may get attacked by wild animals or get bitten by snakes and rodents. They may even catch ticks that could cause Lyme disease.

Dogs may even restrict you from doing certain activities in the campsite. Some areas in national parks do not allow dogs and other pets and thus you might not be able to gain access to such areas if you bring your dog. Dogs may provoke wild animals and cause you to be greatly bothered by them.

Taking your pet dog camping can have its merits and demerits. You have to carefully decide whether to bring your dog or not. If you do so, it is best to check with your dog's veterinarian to make sure that your best friend is fit for the outdoors.

The choice is up to you whether you should bring your dog camping. If you do decide to bring the family dog along, enjoy the moment together, after all, your dog is your best friend!

STAYING IN TOUCH

"There's no wi-fi in the mountains, but you'll find no better connection."
—Unknown

KEEP IN TOUCH EVEN WHEN CAMPING OUT

How should you stay in contact with friends and loved ones when you are outdoors and away from all the amenities and convenience of civilization? Easy, there are various ways and means as well as gear that is available to cater to a camper's every need. The following are tips and advice to make keeping in touch during camping as easy as a-b-c.

SET BOUNDARIES AND FOLLOW THEM

Camping, especially if there are kids around, could be quite a complicated activity. To make it less complex and safe, try to set some boundaries in and around the campsite. Advise campers, especially kid campers, what are the things they should do and not do with or without an adult. Usually, an effective method is requiring kids to always be with a buddy. This could be an assigned partner where one could check in on each other on where the other's location is, or update the rest of the group of any location changes.

FAMILIARIZE YOURSELF WITH THE SURROUNDINGS

Once you arrive in the camp, make sure that you and the campers immediately familiarize yourself with the surroundings. Try to take note of any noticeable landmarks that are around. A large tree perhaps, yet make sure these landmarks are easy to locate in relation to the campsite.

WHISTLE, WHISTLE, WHISTLE

Equip each camper, especially children, with their very own whistle. Establish a code for specific situations that everyone could easily follow and heed. For example, a whistle blown two times could be established to mean "help." Whistles that are blown three times could mean "I am here."

COLOR YOUR WORLD

Or at least, have campers carry trash bags that are colored brightly. Once lost, these bags could be used as a device to signal to the others your location. Also, the bags could be used during an emergency like when it is cold outside and they need temporary shelter. Simply cut a slit at the bag's top and have it pull through the head. Believe it or not, this plastic bag could serve as an effective albeit temporary protection that could keep a kid camper alive through the night.

CHOOSE A CAMP THAT PROVIDES HIGH-TECH COMMUNICATION

This type of camp is perfect for those who might want to be in touch with their business or personal affairs while at the camping grounds. This type of camp strikes a balance between the rugged outdoors and the comfort and convenience of modern technology.

Make use of high-tech communication gear when away from civilization.

If you really want to stay connected, utilize modern technology through the following gear:

Hand-held radios This equipment is very handy now-a-days and so could be easily transportable anywhere and anytime campers need to communicate with each other. Currently though, such equipment is also used not just in camping but also by families that are out shopping or attending a large sports event.

Global positioning system (GPS) Currently, units that have gps are used by the military and units involved in search and rescue operations. Though these devices have features that are high-tech, they are still easy to operate and very user friendly.

Night vision goggles. The movies are not the only place this equipment could be seen and used. These devices are now readily available. Though these are sophisticated, they are very easy to use, light weight and are compact and handy.

All in all, staying in touch while camping may be a bit difficult if you have no idea how to go about it. To be able to avoid this, prepare the equipment, rules and stuff you need to go through beforehand. Camping should be fun. Ample preparation adds to enjoyment and lessens the stress.

The catch to all of these is that coverages where you are will determine if many of these devices will work. Outside of satellite options, most of the time cell services are going to be a challenge. Connect with the campsite manager to determine if and where most people get coverage at the campsite. It's also a good idea to determine if specific carriers get better or worse service on that property.

THE VOYAGE TO THE CAMPSITE

"The voyage of discovery is not in seeking new
landscapes but in having new eyes."
—Marcel Proust

Are we there yet? Are we there yet? Are we there yet? Helpful ways to make them stop with the annoyance! Road trips are fun, during the first hour perhaps. After that everything goes downhill. So how can road trips be fun beginning when the journey starts up until the destination?

The following are tips and advice to help make road trips – especially if it involves kids – fun and happy.

PACK AND PREPARE

As always, prevention is better than cure. Packing and preparing prior to a long road trip must also include planning the activities the kids could do during the ride. Face it, eight-hour drives are difficult for kids. It will not be much help if the stops you make are only at gas stations or during meal times. Keep your kids pre-occupied and entertained at least. And do not forget to pack in some snacks, hopefully some healthy ones, so kids have something to nibble on during the long ride. They are your responsibility and it is you who are taking them for the ride.

RESEARCH, RESEARCH AND RESEARCH

Get to know the road that you are to take prior to you going on the journey. This helps you make the necessary stops and recreational activities that kids may need to pack with them. Stopping at a park or a kids attraction is a good distraction for the long trip ahead.

Another helpful thing is that families must make sure to stay clear from the same old restaurant chains. Food must be special also and it would help if traditional hamburger joints are avoided in favor of specialized and decent road diners.

Depart really late or depart really early when taking A very long road trip. Both options help avoid heavy traffic. Also, the kids are given the time to have some additional sleep, thus keeping them quiet along the road.

STOP IN THE NAME OF LOVE

According to a study, it is highly recommended that stops be made at least every hour or two. This allows your kids to have the necessary breaks. This also allows them to avoid car sickness.

Car sickness could best be avoided by walking around. Kids need to do this to keep their blood circulating during the long trip. Avoid giving motion sickness drugs to kids, as it could keep them unnecessarily sedated.

PACK SOME HANDY BOARD GAMES

Games that are magnetized and could be easily transported anywhere could provide hours of fun. Also, books that have activities in them are good options also. Believe it or not, there is a company that manufactures products and books that are focused on travel. Some of the activities found in these books are crossword puzzles. This is also a good way to make friends on a long journey.

COLLECT STUFF AND MAKE THEM INTO A SCRAPBOOK

Try to encourage children to keep and collect little trinkets found during the journey. Stubs from tickets, brochures and postcards may be kept and be later put into a scrapbook.

BRING DEVICES PRELOADED

Thankfully, your devices have the uncanny ability to keep everyone occupied, at peace and in harmony with each other especially on long trips. Audio books are also a great way to keep kids listening and therefore quiet.

CHILL OUT, SIT BACK AND RELAX

The saying, the journey is better than the destination has never rang true. The memories of a road trip that is filled with activities and good memories are better than thinking of the stress of actually getting there. In the end, it is better to look back with fondness than with frustration.

INVOLVE KIDS IN YOUR TRAVEL PLANS

The trip will actually be best enjoyed by kids more than adults. So as much as possible, get kids to be involved in the planning. Allow them to look at the maps, show them the guidebooks. They would better appreciate the journey if you let them in on what they are getting themselves into. Who knows, they may even suggest helpful tips to make the journey more enjoyable. Never underestimate their wisdom. Rember, a trip is best enjoyed if there is less control and if you just let go and allow things to positively flow.

Closing Thoughts: You have here all you need to enjoy the day in the woods. Now it's up to you. Start planning your trip. Get outside. Breathe the air. Feel the sun. Embrace a simpler version of yourself.

Camping is for Everyone.

APPENDIX 1: AFFIRMATIONS

I END EACH DAY WITH OUTDOOR TIME.

The simple things that I do each day add to my serenity. That includes spending time amidst the beauty of nature. I go outside each evening as part of my therapy.

Inhaling fresh air is refreshing. When I take deep breaths from my patio, I feel my spirit lift. Newness springs into my mind and soul and makes me ready to say goodbye to the day behind me.

I think about the day's experiences and focus on how to use them to extract more value from the next day.

My mind focuses on preparing for tomorrow's wins when I allow it to take in the quietness of the outdoors. Nature has a way of letting me to let go of things that are out of my control. It inspires me to look ahead.

I gain a deep appreciation of my blessing when I spend a few moments each evening in the garden.

CAMPING IS FOR EVERYONE

Observing flowers and plants while welcoming the coolness of the night reminds me to be thankful at all times. It also reminds me to find beauty in each situation that I am a part of. Sometimes downtime is what my mind and body crave.

Being closer to the setting sun allows me to focus on its meaning. Seeing one chapter close without the threat of disaster is reassuring.

It tells me that worry is fruitless. I am urged to live in positive anticipation.

Today, the beauty and tranquility of the outdoors serve as my inspiration. My sense of purpose is renewed when I open myself to the gifts of an ending day.

APPRECIATING THE BEAUTY OF NATURE SUSTAINS ME.

As I walk outside each day, I look around. I inhale the air. I notice the sensation of the breeze across my face. I am struck by the loveliness of the natural environment.

The beauty of nature wraps its arms around me. Today can be my best day or my worst day. No matter which, nature is right there, waiting to guide me through my life.

I feel grateful each time I think about the natural world. Although I believe it will always be there for me, I still gasp in sheer joy when I see deep purple blooms on the bushes or snowflakes falling from the sky.

The rich, green grass of summer tickles my nose with its aroma. This entices me to linger outdoors a few minutes more.

If a troubling thought nags at my mind, I take a walk in the open air. I breathe in, I breathe out. The aromas of nature and the caress of the breeze rise up to meet me. Each time, I find what I need to continue with my day.

When I am outdoors, I momentarily forget about the stresses of life. Any unsettling feelings I am experiencing dissolve. I am sustained by nature's sweet song.

Today, I promise to take intimate notice of nature's backdrop. The color of the sky, the faint fragrance in the air, and the sound of the trees rustling in the breeze all call out to me. The beauty of nature, ever-present, sustains me.

HIKING IS EXHILARATING TO ME.

Working out sometimes feels like a chore but I am committed to it. I choose exercise that increases my energy. Taking hikes exhilarates me, so I include them in my weekly workout routine.

I practice fitness at the gym during the week, but I go for long, early morning hikes during the weekend.

The scenery is uplifting. It is refreshing to feel my body work as I absorb the beauty of the natural environment around me. Challenging slopes are manageable because I am breathing fresh air.

I look forward to getting to the top of a mountain. I feel proud of myself each time I accomplish that feat without quitting.

It is also breathtaking to fill my nostrils with the scent of greenery and my lungs with clean air. My body hardly notices the wear it undergoes as I take in the moment at the top of the slope.

The views from that vantage point are spectacular. They urge me to take a moment to be thankful for the blessings of nature.

Seeing the treetops in their wonder reminds me to hold my head up. I feel proud of who I am when I see tall trees beaming above everything else. They are my inspiration to ignore the opinions of others and let my brightest light shine.

Today, I appreciate hiking for both its health benefits and its ability to connect me to my inner greatness. It is inspiring to take on a climbing challenge in the midst of nature that nullifies any other choice but perseverance.

BREATH

Take your next breath in slowly and release it intentionally.
I choose to make happiness my number one goal in life.
The things in my life I do not like I can either accept or change.
I let go of the tension that is within me with every breath.
I am open to a deep calmness inside me.
I am what I think so I choose to think positive thoughts.
I release all thoughts that do not serve me well.
I'm making every effort to forgive myself and others.

APPENDIX 2: FOOD BASICS AND RECIPES

Consider keeping some slow-to-perish items in your camping food bin to use throughout the camping season, supplementing with other perishable ingredients as needed—don't forget the marshmallows! Here are just a few suggestions to get you started, but adapt the list to fit your needs.

- Salt & pepper
- Spices
- Cooking oil/nonstick spray
- Coffee/tea/hot chocolate
- Sweeteners (sugar, honey, sugar substitute)
- Oatmeal
- Pancake mix
- Syrup
- Rice
- Dried pasta
- Canned foods (soup, chili, etc.)
- Dried foods (fruit, jerky, etc.)
- Energy foods (bars, gels, trail mix)
- Peanut butter
- Jelly/jam

CAMPING RECIPES

Ocean Packets

Prep: 30 mins
Cook: 15 mins
Total: 45 mins
Servings: 8

Ingredient Checklist

- ½ cup unsalted butter, melted
- 1 tablespoon grated fresh lemon peel
- 32 clams in shell, scrubbed
- 32 uncooked shrimp, deveined but with shells
- 32 sea scallops
- 8 ears corn on the cob, cut into quarters
- 32 large cherry tomatoes
- 8 12x12-inch squares aluminum foil
- 1 tablespoon chopped fresh chives

If you can't find clams, use mussels. If someone doesn't care for clams, double up on the shrimp and/or scallops. Baking times may vary according to the ingredients you select.

Directions

- **Step 1**
  Preheat an outdoor grill for medium heat, and lightly oil the grate. Mix the butter with lemon peel in a bowl.

- **Step 2**
  Spread out the sheets of foil onto a flat work surface, and place 4 clams, 4 shrimp, 4 scallops, 4 pieces of corn on the cob, and 4 cherry tomatoes in the center of each piece of foil. Drizzle 1 tablespoon of lemon-butter mixture over the seafood and vegetables. Bring two opposite ends of a foil sheet together and fold over several times to seal. Leave room for steam. Fold the remaining ends over several times to seal the packet completely.

- **Step 3**
  Place the foil packets on the preheated grill, cover the grill, and bake until the clams are open and the shrimp are pink and opaque, 15 to 20 minutes (open a packet a little to take a peek).

- **Step 4**
  To serve, place a foil packet on a plate, cut a diagonal X through the foil, and peel back the foil. Garnish each packet with about 1/2 teaspoon of chives.

Foil Barbecued Trout with Wine

Prep: 15 mins
Cook: 20 mins
Total: 35 mins
Servings: 2

Ingredient Checklist

- 2 trout, cleaned and head removed

- ¼ cup dry white wine
- 2 tablespoons butter, melted
- 1 tablespoon lemon juice
- 2 tablespoons chopped fresh parsley
- salt and pepper to taste

Directions

- **Step 1**
  Get the grill hot enough to produce medium to high heat.

- **Step 2**
  On a flat surface, lay out two sheets of aluminum foil about 18 inches long so that they overlap to make one long wide sheet. Rinse the trout and pat dry. Lay the fish in the center of the foil about 2 inches apart. Sprinkle it with white wine, melted butter and lemon juice. Season with parsley, salt and pepper. Fold the foil up loosely around the fish and crimp the seams to seal.

- **Step 3**
  Place the packet on the grill and cook for 15 to 20 minutes, or until fish is cooked through.

Simple Grilled Lamb Chops

Prep: 10 mins
Cook: 6 mins
Additional: 2 hrs
Total: 2 hrs 16 mins
Servings: 6

Ingredient Checklist

- ¼ cup distilled white vinegar
- 2 teaspoons salt
- ½ teaspoon black pepper
- 1 tablespoon minced garlic
- 1 onion, thinly sliced
- 2 tablespoons olive oil
- 2 pounds lamb chops

Directions

- **Step 1**
  Prepare your marinade at home. Mix together the vinegar, salt, pepper, garlic, onion, and olive oil in a large resealable bag until the salt has dissolved. Add lamb, toss until coated, and marinate in a cooler for 2 hours.

- **Step 2**
  Preheat the grill for medium-high heat.

- **Step 3**
  Remove lamb from the marinade and leave any onions on that stick to the meat. Discard any remaining marinade. Wrap the exposed ends of the bones with aluminum foil to keep them from burning. Grill to desired doneness, about 3 minutes per side for medium.

Muffin Pan Eggs on the Grill

Prep: 10 mins
Cook: 6-8 mins
Servings: 12

Ingredient Checklist

For the scrambled egg pancetta:

- Free Range Eggs, lightly scrambled
- White onions, diced
- Pancetta, lightly sautéed
- Freshly ground black pepper to taste

For the vegetarian:

- Free Range Eggs
- Fresh spinach, chopped
- Tomatoes, diced
- Shredded white cheese blend
- Garlic, minced

For the ham and mushroom:

- Free Range Eggs
- Mushrooms, diced
- Ham, diced
- Green onions, sliced

For the bacon and cheddar:

- Free Range Eggs
- Bacon, cooked and diced
- Bell peppers, diced
- Cheddar cheese, shredded

Directions

- **Step 1**
  Preheat grill

- **Step 2**
  Grease muffin pan. Crack an egg in each muffin compartment. If making the scrambled egg pancetta, lightly beat the egg after cracking it into the muffin pan.

- **Step 3**
  Sprinkle the remaining ingredients for the type of muffin you're making over the top of each egg. You can make all four recipes or just pick your favorite one! Ingredient amounts will depend on how many you make of each muffin type.

- **Step 4**
  Carefully place entire muffin pan on grill and cook for 6-8 minutes. Check periodically and use a fork or butter knife to remove egg muffins from muffin pan when whites are set and yolks are cooked to your liking.

Perfectly Grilled Steak

Prep: 15 mins
Cook: 15 mins

Ingredient Checklist

- (4) 1 1/4-to-1 1/2-inch-thick boneless rib-eye or New York strip steaks (about 12 ounces each) or filets mignons (8 to 10 ounces each), trimmed
- 2 tablespoons canola or extra-virgin olive oil
- Kosher salt and freshly ground pepper

Directions

- **Step 1**
  About 20 minutes before grilling, remove the steaks from the cooler and let sit, covered.

- **Step 2**
  Heat your grill up. Brush the steaks on both sides with oil and season liberally with salt and pepper. Place the steaks on the grill and cook until golden brown and slightly charred, 4 to 5 minutes. Turn the steaks over and continue to grill 3 to 5 minutes for medium-rare (an internal temperature of 135 degrees F), 5 to 7 minutes for medium (140 degrees F) or 8 to 10 minutes for medium-well (150 degrees F).

- **Step 3**
  Transfer the steaks to a cutting board or platter, tent loosely with foil and let rest 5 minutes before slicing

Campfire Chicken Under a Brick with Lemons

Prep: 10 mins
Total: 50 mins
Servings: 4

Ingredient Checklist

- 1 whole chicken (about 4 pounds)
- 1/4 cup plus 1 tablespoon extra-virgin olive oil
- Coarse salt and freshly ground pepper
- 2 lemons, cut into wedges
- Pinch of crushed red-pepper flakes

Directions

- **Step 1**
  Remove backbone from chicken using kitchen shears. Place chicken, breast side up, on a cutting board, with legs extended on both sides. Press firmly on breastbone to break it and flatten chicken. Rub all over with 2 tablespoons oil, and season generously with salt and pepper.

- **Step 2**
  Heat 2 tablespoons oil in a cast-iron skillet set over a campfire or on a medium grill. Place chicken in skillet, breast side down, and place a clean brick or heavy skillet directly on top, pressing to flatten chicken. Grill until skin is golden and crisp, about 12 minutes.

- **Step 3**
  Remove brick, and flip chicken. Cover with foil, and grill for 20 minutes more. Flip chicken, and grill until cooked through and an instant-read thermometer inserted into the thigh reaches 165 degrees, about 5 minutes more.

- **Step 4**
  Meanwhile, grill lemon wedges directly on grates, flipping, until caramelized, about 2 minutes per side. Transfer chicken to a platter. Drizzle with remaining tablespoon oil, and sprinkle with red-pepper flakes. Serve with lemons.

No-oven Pizza

Prep: 10 mins
Cook: 30 mins
Easy
Serves 4

Ingredient Checklist

- 1 cup self-raising flour
- 3 tbsp olive oil , plus extra for frying

For the topping

- 1 tsp olive oil
- 1 onion , sliced
- 3 garlic cloves , crushed
- 250g pack cherry tomatoes , halved
- 4 tbsp passata
- handful fresh basil leaves , chopped
- ⅓ Cup cheddar (Cheese of choice) , grated

Directions

- **Step 1**

  Heat the oil in a frying pan attop your grill. Then add the onion and garlic and cook for 5 mins. Tip in tomatoes and passata, and simmer for 5-10 mins or until the tomatoes are soft. Remove from the heat, stir in the basil, season, then allow to cool.

- **Step 2**

  Put the flour into a bowl. Make a whole in the middle, add the olive oil then add 6-7 tbsp warm water or enough to make a soft dough. Tip the dough onto a lightly floured surface and roll out to fit a 9 inch frying pan or make 2 small ones. Heat a glug of olive oil in the frying pan, then press the dough into the pan and cook over a medium heat for 8-10 mins or until the base is golden.

- **Step 3**

  Heat grill to hot. Spread the pizza base with the tomato sauce, scatter on the cheese and grill until it has melted and the base is golden at the edges. Serve immediately.

TIPS FOR TELLING A GREAT CAMPFIRE STORY

Tell a story that you enjoy. Telling good stories isn't just about entertaining. This is your opportunity to share bits of wisdom. Create a hook. Use props, get the listeners to use their imaginations, interact with them by playing on their senses and the environment. Keep their attention by making the story short and sweet. Don't rush through it, use dramatic pauses. Be flexible, each audience is different. If one thing doesn't work, don't be afraid to switch it up! This will ensure that everyone enjoys your campfire stories and remembers them for years to come

Do not Visit Lover's Lane

A young couple went to the movies, and stopped at the local Lover's Lane for some kissing. The boy turned on the radio to set the mood. Just as he reaches his arms around his girlfriend, a news bulletin warns of an escaped murderer who has a hook for a right hand. The man had escaped from a facility for the criminally insane.

The boy thinks it will be funny to tease his girlfriend to scare her. He begins to tell her he is sure they are in a place the escapee might choose to hide. He goes on and on terrifying his girlfriend. He hoped she would throw herself into his arms for comfort, however his plan backfires. His girlfriend insists they leave right away.

Reluctantly, the boy drives his girlfriend home. When she gets out, she begins yelling and faints. The young man jumps out and runs around the car. There, on her door handle, is a bloody hook!

The Unheeded Warning

A young lady was driving home after a long vacation. Sometime after midnight, a very heavy storm begins as she notices she is almost out of gas. She sees a sign for a gas station and convenience store and pulls off the interstate to fill her tank. The place is obviously open, but deserted, run-down, and old. She almost drives on, but concerned she might run out of gas, decides to stop and just get gas. As she pulls in, a tall man with a badly scarred face comes running through the rain. He pumps her gas and the girl rolls her window down just enough to hand him her credit card. He grabs it and runs back inside.

The scarred man comes back, tells her she will have to come inside, because her card was denied, and hurries back inside without allowing her to respond. She really doesn't want to go inside and considers driving off without paying. However, she decides to go in very quickly, take care of the bill, and leave as soon as possible.

When she gets inside, the man grabs her arm and tries to talk to her. His voice is rough and difficult to understand and she thinks he may have had his voice damaged in whatever accident scarred his face. The man gets increasingly excited and the young girl becomes more frantic. She finally wrests herself from his grip and runs back to her car, leaving the station as quickly as possible. She sees the old man through her back window yelling and gesturing her to come back, but she keeps driving.

She turns on the radio to help her relax and sees something move behind her. She looks in the rear-view mirror, just as a man appears in the back seat holding an ax. That is the last thing she sees in this life. The scarred man at the gas station had been trying to warn her.

The Killer Under the Bed

A young girl's parents were going out for the night. Although she was still young, she thought she was too old for a babysitter. She begs to be allowed to stay home alone, even though her parents will be out very late. She promises to go to bed at her regular bed time and calls her parents on her cell phone just before she settles down for the night to tell them she is fine and not to wake her when they come home. She will see them in the morning.

She is almost asleep when she hears dripping noises. She gets up to see if it is raining outside, but the star and moon are shining brightly. She returns to bed, and as she closes her eyes, she hears the dripping noise again. Her hand is hanging out of bed and she takes comfort when she feels a wet tongue lick it. Knowing their dog is under her bed provides comfort. The dripping noise continues and she finally decides she must know what it is.

The young girl gets up and turns on the light. The noise continues and she keeps looking for the source. (At this point, the narrator can stretch the story out, describing various places where she looks, i.e. the hallway, the adjacent bathroom – sink and shower, etc.) Finally, she looks in her closet. There hangs her dog, dripping blood, with a note that says, "Humans lick, too."

CAMPFIRE GHOST STORIES

Is there anything scarier than a ghost story? Perhaps it is because we all think spectral beings might possibly exist. Not all ghosts are malevolent, but they are all terrifying, and so are these stories.

The Ghost of Rest Haven

Aunt Lacy loved taking her niece, Felicity, on day trips. One of their favorite destinations was the beach. One summer day the air was particularly refreshing and the water a perfect temperature for wading. Aunt Lacy and Felicity became enamored with the little creatures they were finding in the tide pools, and all at once realized that not only was the sun setting, but it looked as if a very bad thunderstorm was coming. They quickly got in the car to head home.

The storm was worse than Lacy had thought and she was afraid to keep driving. She decided to pull off the road until the storm passed, but just as she was about to do so, Felicity declared, "Look! There's a place we can stay."

Sure enough, Lacy saw a sign on a large house, "Rest Haven – Rooms for Rent – Day, Week, Month." Feeling relieved, Lacy pulled in, parked, and they both ran to the porch as quickly as possible. A white-haired woman answered the door before they could even knock. She said, "I have been expecting you."

Although this seemed odd to Lacy, the woman had a pleasant smile, so she pushed her feeling of unease to the back of her mind and smiled back. The old woman gave them a hot meal and showed them to a warm, cozy room. The furniture was old and worn, but clean.

When they awoke in the morning, they were eager to head home. There was no cell phone reception at the old house and

Lacy was sure Felicity's mom must be frantic with worry. They wanted to thank the proprietor, but she was nowhere to be found. They left a note taped to the door-jam with some money for their stay and left.

A few miles down the road, Aunt Lacy's phone beeped, indicating she had a message or call. She stopped at a country gas station to call Felicity's mom and tell her they were on their way and okay. Lacy decided to fill her tank and buy some drinks. While paying for the gas and drinks, she made conversation with the attendant, telling him about their enjoyable stay at Rest Haven. Looking surprised, the man told Lacy and Felicity that the home had burned down years ago, killing the owner.

They could not believe what they had been told, so headed back to see. There was no house, but on the ground, lay their note and the money.

A Final Performance

Callie was extremely tired and stopped at an old house with a sign declaring, "The Oaks Inn – Bed and Breakfast." The room was very comfortable and she fell asleep as soon as she lay down on the bed. Callie woke up in the wee hours of the morning to the sound of a pianist playing Beethoven's Moonlight Sonata.

Callie was a pianist herself, traveling to the next town for a concert, and was very impressed with the skill of whoever was playing. She glanced at the clock and wondered who and why someone would be playing the piano at 2:00 in the morning. She simply could not go back to sleep while the music was playing. She finally decided she must ask whoever was playing the music to stop so she could get some sleep.

As she entered the dining room on the first floor of the inn, she saw a man seated at a piano in the corner. He was extremely handsome and dressed in a tuxedo. With his thin mustache and slicked-back hair, he looked like someone from the roaring twenties. The man looked at her and said, "Well, Callie, here you are. I have been waiting for you for a long time." Callie was surprised that he knew her name, but felt enchanted by his tone of voice. When she made no reply – for she was quite speechless – he spoke again. "Come sit with me, Callie."

Unable to resist his command, Callie moved to the piano and sat next to the man. "Now, Callie, play with me."

Callie felt a chill in the air and shivered. Unable to resist the man's command, she placed her fingers on the piano and they began to play the sonata together. As they played, they both faded out of sight as the music became softer and softer. At the last moment before completely disappearing, Callie realized she had just played her last performance.

Prom Night

Johnny left his friend's house late at night and headed home down the dark country roads. It began to rain. Suddenly, Johnny saw the blurry image of a woman in a long, white dress walking down the middle of the road. Johnny had to stop, so he asked the young woman if she needed a ride. Without saying anything, she got in and sat in the front seat. Since she was shivering, Johnny took off his coat and put it over her shoulders.

After a few miles, the girl indicated, again without speaking, that she needed to get out at an old house. Johnny stopped the car and the girl opened the door. Johnny rolled down the window to ask for his coat, but the girl was gone.

He left his car and walked to the door. An older woman answered and he explained that he had forgotten to get his jacket from the young woman he had just dropped off at the house. The woman began crying and explained to Johnny that her daughter, on this evening ten years previously, was on the way to her Prom when she was killed in a car accident. She was buried in the cemetery up the road, in the exact spot where Johnny had picked her up.

The next day, Johnny drove to the cemetery to confirm the woman's story. There, on the grave of a young girl, was Johnny's jacket.

Tombstone Terror

Alan and Matt were ghost hunters. They would visit old cemeteries and see if they could stir up a spirit from an old tombstone. They set up their recorder on a particularly large and ornate headstone and prepared to begin. They were afraid to shine their flashlights on the stone to see the name engraved there, as trespassing in the cemetery at night was illegal. They had crawled over the fence at the rear of the cemetery to avoid the caretaker.

Matt flipped the on button on the recorder and said aloud, "We would like to speak to whoever lies beneath this stone." In response, all they heard was the scratching noise that seemed to come from behind the tombstone.

With a calm voice Alan said, "Please tell us your name."

Again, the only response was a scratching noise, so Matt said, "We only wish to speak with you. Please show yourself."

Suddenly, both young men felt the air turn cold, and a tall, dark shadow rose from behind the tombstone. The shadow moved to engulf them. Alan and Matt had many encounters with spirits, and were not afraid. Too late, they both realized the apparition meant them harm. The shadow swept down, engulfing them, and pulled them into the ground beneath the tombstone.

The next morning, the caretaker of the cemetery found the recorder on the ground by the tombstone. He turned it on, and after each question, he heard the following response: "Yes…I am here."

"My name is never spoken by the living."

"If I show myself, it will be the last thing you will ever see."

"I got you both!"

The caretaker quietly picked up the recorder. Knowing he had the only evidence that someone had been in the cemetery and by that tombstone, he went to his tool shed and tossed the recorder into a pile with many others.

KIDS STORIES

The Unstoppable Coffin - (Funny - Stories for all ages)

One day a South Carolina man decided to go camping at Yosemite. He had a great weekend but when it was time to go home, he realized his car's battery had died. Since he lived nearby, the man decided to walk the three hours home and call a tow-truck in the morning.

After an hour of walking, the sun went down, but the man wasn't worried. Soon he passed a cemetery and began to whistle as he walked to avoid feeling nervous. But not long after he began whistling, he heard a Bump, Bump, Bump behind him.

At first, the man walked faster, but the bumping sped up too! Bump, Bump, Bump, Bump. The man looked over his shoulder and was terrified to see a giant upright coffin hopping after him. Bump, Bump, Bump.

The man ran. The coffin continued to bump behind him. As he passed someone's trash can, the man hurled the can behind him into the coffin. The coffin tipped over and the man ran away as he thought he was safe. Not so! Soon he heard the Bump, Bump, Bump again and there was the coffin. Right behind him.

Finally, the man got home. He hurled his own trash can at the coffin. Nothing. It followed him up the steps, and onto the porch. He tried to slam the door but it crashed right through.

The man threw a chair at the coffin, but that barely slowed it down. At last, it cornered him in the bathroom. Desperately, he grabbed a bottle of cough syrup and threw it. It broke and splattered all over the wooden lid. It was only then that the coffin stopped.

The Ghost With One Black Eye – (Funny – Stories for all ages)

In the early 1900s, there existed a tavern on the road that went from the countryside to the city. Travelers would stop there to eat and rest. The entire tavern would be full except for one haunted room.

Years ago, a fight at the tavern left a man with a severe blow to one eye. As he fainted, the others at the tavern placed him in that room. He never recovered and died in the room. Since then his ghost seemed to haunt that room.

One day a cowboy came to the tavern. The old owner told him that there was no room except the haunted one.

The cowboy said, "I rope bulls and wrestle with them every day. I ain't afraid of any ghost," and took the room. That night during a bath, the cowboy heard a booming voice, "I am the ghost with one black eye."

The cowboy panicked and looked around to find none. He wrapped his towel and ran as fast as he could.

Another day, a barmaid came for a room but the tavern was full. The old man said that there was only one room left and it was haunted.

The barmaid said, "I have seen the most violent of men at the place where I work. No ghost can scare me. I will take the room."

That night, while tucking into the bed, she heard the same words in the booming voice. A shiver ran down her spine. She wore her gown, picked her luggage, and dashed out of the tavern.

A few days later, came a couple with a son. The couple wanted a separate room for themselves, but the only other room available for the son was haunted.

The son said, "Cool, a real ghost. I will live in it!"

That night, when the boy switched off the lights to go to bed, he heard the voice, "I am the ghost with one black eye." The young boy calmly switched on the bed lamp and said, "Well, I am a boy scout. If you do not keep your mouth shut, you will be a ghost with two black eyes."

After that, it was totally silent. The boy switched off the light and slept peacefully. Since that day, the ghost never disturbed or scared anyone again.

The New Baby Sister (Scary - Stories for older kids)

Once upon a time, there was a loving couple and their young daughter who lived in a tiny apartment in North Carolina. They were very happy but their one unfulfilled dream was to live in a big house with room for even more children. They worked hard to save up enough money for a big house and every day, their daughter begged for a baby sister.

"Mamma" she'd cry, "why can't I have a little sister?"

"We want to give you a sister, sweetie," Said her mother. "But first we have to buy a big house so there's room for everyone!"

Finally, they had enough money and bought a big beautiful old house in the Blue Ridge Mountains where they had always wanted to live. The house was perfect with big curving staircases, a basement, an attic, and even a nursery for the little sister their daughter had always wanted. What they didn't know was why the house was so affordable. An entire family just like theirs had died there years before, including a little girl only a few years younger than their daughter.

As much as the couple loved their new house, their daughter loved it more. She loved to explore and ventured into every room, except the basement where her mother told her not to go. But every night, the little girl heard a faint whisper

"I'm in the basement," the whisper said. "Come to the basement. I'm in the basement".

Every night the girl heard this whisper. It scared her, at first. But soon, her curiosity was too much to resist.

"Come to the basement" it whispered, and so she crept out of her bed. The ghostly voice guided her. "I'm in the basement" it whispered.

The next morning, her mother awoke to find their daughter missing! They checked every room in the house. The kitchen, the nursery, even the attic. But she was nowhere to be found. Finally, the mother ventured into the basement to find her little girl sitting on the floor talking to no one.

The girl was sitting in front of an ancient dusty toy chest and in her hands was a porcelain doll in a faded lace dress. When the girl heard her mother, she looked up and smiled.

"Momma, momma!" she cried. "I finally have a baby sister!"

The living couple's daughter had befriended the ghost of the girl who died there years before.

Little Johnny and the Scarecrow (Scary – Stories for older kids)

Seven-year-old Johnny loved spending time at his grandfather's farmhouse. It was an old-fashioned place with huge farmland at the front, a barn, and a sheep's pen by the side of the house, and a scarecrow.

Johnny loved the scarecrow. He drew a smile on it and called it Fluffy. Little Johnny also loved spending time at the sheep enclosure. He had helped his grandpa hammer the wooden planks together to make the sheep's pen. Life was fun at the farmhouse.

One evening, Johnny decided to go ride his bike along the trail beside the Choctawhatchee Bay. He was so busy that he did not realize that the clouds at the horizon had turned into a thunderstorm. The rain lashed out across the bay and Johnny could barely see the road. "Where am I?" thought Johnny. His confusion turned into fear and he started crying. Suddenly he felt a hand on his shoulder. Johnny turned and it was a tall man. The rain was so heavy that Johnny could barely see the man's face, but could tell that he was a jolly person with a cap on his head.

"Are you lost?" said the man.

"Yes, sir."

"Okay, I know the way back to where you live. Come." The man took Johnny's hand, while Johnny pulled his bike with another.

Soon the duo reached Johnny's farmhouse. Johnny could tell it was grandpa's place by the outline of the house that he could see through the haze of the heavy rain.

"Go Johnny. That is your place, isn't it?" said the man.

"Yes, sir! Thank you, sir!"

Johnny hurried towards the main entrance while the man stood at a distance. Johnny dropped his bike when suddenly there was a roar of thunder behind him. It tripped Johnny. He turned around and got the shock of his life. Lightning had fallen on the man and now he was engulfed in flames. The rainwater evaporated as steam, as the man hovered at his place about to collapse. Johnny screamed at the top of his voice. Grandpa rushed out of the house and pulled Johnny inside.

The next morning was bright and sunny. The entire family stepped out to take stock of the damage. The sheep were safe in the barn, but their pen was destroyed. Johnny's bicycle was safe too. There was no sign of the man although there was a mark of lightning on the soil. As Johnny looked around, he heard his grandpa gasp. Johnny rushed towards grandpa who was staring at something on the land. Johnny looked as well. On the ground lay Fluffy, the scarecrow, dismembered with his parts charred black; burnt like when lightning strikes something.

The Mysterious Firewood Ghost (Scary – Stories for all ages)

Not so long ago, there was a group of campers in Pine Mountain, Georgia.Campers just like you.They had planned to camp out all week long and had been dropped off by their parents, so there was no car to get home with. They thought it would be great! But on the very first night, a terrible storm blew through their camp. Whoosh!

The wind blew away all their supplies. It blew away their firewood, their food, their backpacks, even the muddy hiking boots they'd placed outside their tents. Everything!

In the morning, the campers looked around at the wrecked camp and realized they were stranded in the woods for a week with almost no supplies. They tried to collect what was scattered around, but there wasn't enough food or firewood to get them through the week, and without their hiking boots, they couldn't go far from the campsite. And because of the storm, all the nearby fallen wood was too soaked to burn.

The second night, they crawled into their tents hungry and tried to sleep. One boy named Thomas woke up in the middle of the night to the sound of someone moving around outside and an eerie light coming through his tent. Thomas was so terrified of the strange light and sound that it took him ten whole minutes before he peeked out of his tent to see who it was.But no one was there!

The next morning, the campers discovered that their cooler was back and had an unopened package of hotdogs inside next to a little pile of mysteriously dry firewood. The campers were confused, but they rejoiced and quickly set up a delicious weenie roast breakfast.

The third night, they crawled into their tents and fell into a deep sleep. But again, Thomas was woken up in the middle of the night by the sound of someone moving around and an eerie light outside his tent. Again, he felt terrified, but eventually peeked out to see if it was a friend with a flashlight.

No one was there!

In the morning, they found their backpacks dry and tidily packed outside their tents along with their loaf of bread and block of cheese along with another little pile of dry firewood. Delighted, but confused, the group had breakfast and played card games from a deck of cards found in one of the packs.

On the fourth night, they crawled into their tents and fell asleep. Again, Thomas woke up to a sound and an eerie light. This time, he peeked out immediately to see the glowing figure of a young boy his own age running off into the woods.

In the morning, they discovered their hiking boots dry and clean of mud set outside their tents, a few cans of stew, and more dry firewood. And this time, Thomas had a plan. Lacing up his boots, Thomas set out in the direction he'd seen the glowing figure run the night before.

Soon he came to a deep ravine and peering far, far down into the crevice, he could see a tattered backpack and an ancient pair of shoes. Their mysterious helper had been the ghost of a lost camper the whole time!

A Tired Piece of String (Funny - Stories for all Ages)

A tired piece of string had been traveling in the wilderness for days. He had struggled up craggy trails, passed through lush woodlands, seen thrilling vistas, and slept under breath-taking starlit skies.

As his journey was nearing its end, he passed by the only bar he'd seen. Not wanting to forgo the opportunity to slake his thirst with an ice-cold beverage, he opened the door and stepped inside.

As the string approached the bar, the bartender looked at him and said "You have to leave, we don't serve strings here!" Dejected and disheartened, the string turned around and walked out.

Not one to fail for lack of trying, the string stood outside thinking for a moment. Then he hastily fluffed up his hair, looped himself a few times, and walked back in.

When the bartender saw him the second time, he was puzzled. Although he had changed his appearance slightly, he still looked generally the same. Glaring down at him, the bartender demanded, "Are you a string?!" to which the string replied, "Nope, I'm a frayed knot."

ACKNOWLEDGEMENTS

Dorthy Weston - Grandma I thank you. I love you.

Reese Bessinger - Brother thank you for helping me begin this journey.

Simone Hughes - You can read my mind even when I can't. I thank you.

Ariel Driskell - Thank you for the work on this book. I'm happy that our conversations moved us to this.

Jonathan C Weston - Thank you for being my inspiration to always learn more.

Ayden Weston - Thank you for being my inspiration to be more social and learn more about other people.

Kennedy Weston - Thank you for inspiring me to learn how to love.

Ethan Weston - Thank you for helping me to see that gentle masculinity is the way forward.

Camryn Grace - Thank you for helping me learn forgiveness.

GLOSSARY OF TERMS

A

A-frame: A basic tent shape, the cross section of which resembles an "A".

Altimeter: An instrument that measures elevation by using barometric (air) pressure.

Anorak: A pullover jacket. Anoraks are practical because there is no zipper running top to bottom that can fail or let your body warmth escape when moving.

Azimuth: Same as bearing. Refers to the degree of bearing from your current position to a landmark or destination. Reversing the bearing would be known as a back azimuth or back bearing.

B

Back tack: A stitch sewn over a stitch to reinforce highly stressed areas where two pieces of fabric must be joined. Good quality tents use back-tack stitching.

Baffle construction: A design that keeps the filling in a sleeping bag or outerwear garment from shifting back and forth and causing cold spots. Baffles, or sewn box cavities, can vary in size, shape, and volume within the same garment or bag.

Baseplate: The see-through plate of an orienting compass onto which the compass housing is mounted.

Bathtub floor: In tents, a floor that curves upward at its perimeter and is joined to the canopy. Bathtub floors keep stitching away from ground moisture, thus adding to a tent's waterproofness.

Bear bag: In bear country, campers must take measures to safeguard their food and cooking utensils. Food items are placed in a strong, waterproof bag (the bear bag), tied to a rope and suspended out of reach.

Billy: A small cooking pot with a handle on top, used for cooking food for one to three people.

Bivouac: The site where a tent is set up; also a forced camp usually made for one night when bad weather stops progress.

Bivy sack: A small one-man tent or bag of sleeping bag proportions often used for emergency shelter.

Blaze: A sign, painted symbol on a tree or a rock cairn used to mark a trail.

Boardwalk: A wooden bridge providing walkways along a trail or beach. Boardwalks are typically built to protect fragile areas from hikers or to protect hikers from waterways and wildlife.

Boondocking (RV term): (or dry camping) is a type of camping by an RVer. Camping in this manner involves using a all the self-contained facilities of an RV and without the use of electric, sewer or water hookups

Bushwhacking: Making one's way through bushes or undergrowth without the aid of a formal trail.

C

Cache: A placement of food and/or supplies along or near a trail or route of travel for future use.

Cairn: A stack of rocks used to mark a trail's route through areas devoid of trees.

Canopy: The inner wall of a double-walled tent. The canopy is breathable; the outer wall, or fly, is waterproof.

Cardinal points: The four main points of direction on a compass—North/360 degrees; East/90 degrees; South/180 degrees; and West/270 degrees

Compression stuff sack: A stuff sack with cinch straps that compress the sleeping bag or pad inside so it's small enough to carry easily inside an internal frame pack and minimizes the overall volume within the pack.

Conduction: The loss of body heat through direct contact with a cold surface, damp clothing, cold water, etc.

Convection: Loss of body heat due to wind or other conditions that circulate cold air in exchange for the warm air your body has heated. The body will continuously attempt to warm the skin that is cooled by the cold air, causing you to lose your body heat and become hypothermic.

Cordura: A high-tenacity, abrasion and tear resistant textured yarn used for backpacks and tough duffle bags.

Corduroy: A road, trail or bridge formed by logs laid transversely, side by side, to facilitate crossing swampy areas.

D

Daypack: Small backpack that holds enough gear for a one-day outing.

Deadman: A log or rock buried in the ground to provide a solid point for anchoring a tent in ground too soft for stakes.

Declination: The difference in degrees between magnetic north (the direction the magnetic needle on a compass points) and true or geographic north (the direction maps are printed towards).

Deep-lugged sole: A boot sole featuring deep ridges and grooves for maximum traction.

Denier (den-year): A weight measurement used to refer to the fineness of a yarn or thread used in some backpacking and camping equipment. The lower the denier, the more thin the thread. The higher the denier the more durable the fabric will be.

Dome: A tent shape where the poles create a dome by curving over each other.

Double blaze: Two painted blazes or markings on a tree that announce a change in direction or junction along a trail.

Double-wall construction: A style of tent architecture utilizing two walls—an inner wall, or canopy, made of breathable nylon, and an outer waterproof wall or fly.

Down: The soft, fluffy underlayer of waterfowl plumage used as insulation in some sleeping bags and coats.

Draft tube: The insulated flap that covers the length of a sleeping bag zipper. Without a great draft tube, cold air would be sucked in and warm air forced out every time you moved.

Dry Camping: See "Boondocking"

DWR: Acronym for Durable Water-Repellent finish, a treatment found on outerwear that forces water to bead much as wax does for a car.

E

Encapsulation technology: A special durable water-repellent finish (DWR) that wraps around each fabric fiber, as opposed to going on like a continuous coat of paint. Provides excellent water-repellency, doesn't compromise breathability, is abrasion-proof, adds tear strength, and makes garments feel soft and supple. Used in some down and Polarguard 3D-insulated clothes.

External frame pack: A backpack supported by a rigid frame on the outside of the pack.

F

Floor area: The amount of usable floor space in a tent, measured in square feet.

Foot: The rounded end of a sleeping bag, also called a footbox.

Footprint: The shape and square footage of a tent floor.

Four-season tent: A tent designed to handle any weather conditions, including harsh winter weather.

Freestanding tent: A tent that does not require stakes or guy lines to stand erect.

G

Gaiter: A water-repellent, internal sleeve that can be tightened around boot and lower leg to keep out snow.

Gear loft: An overhead shelf in a tent. Keeps small gear overhead, providing more floor space for bags.

Giardia: More properly known as giardiasis, an infection of the lower intestines caused by ingesting the amoebic cyst, Giardia lamblia, in untreated water.

Ground stakes: Anchors that hold a tent to the ground.

Gusseted tongue (bellows): A leather piece attached to both sides of the upper on a hiking boot, designed to keep out water and dirt.

Guy point: One of several points outside a tent where a line (a guy line) can be attached and then secured to a stake or other anchor in order to increase a tent's structural integrity.

H

Haversack: A bag or pouch used by hikers to carry food, usually carried at the side by a shoulder strap.

Head gasket: A piece sewn around the hood of a sleeping bag to keep in warm air.

Hip belt: The main support device on a backpack. Large padded belt that buckles around the waist and is fully adjustable.

Housing: The rotating part of a compass that holds the damping fluid, the magnetic needle and has degrees engraved around its edge from 1 to 360. Also known as the Azimuth Ring.

I

Imu: A shallow pit used for cooking.

Internal frame pack: A backpack supported by stays on the inside.

J

Junction: The point at which two trails intersect.

Jello-mold: An oven made from a large ring aluminum Jello mold

K

Kerf: A cut made by an ax, saw, etc.

Kindling: Small, thin, dead wood used to start a fire.

L

Lean-to: A three-sided shelter with an over-hanging roof and one open side.

Leave No Trace: A camping/outdoor concept that adheres to a strict policy which means visitors will not leave trash along trails or campsites to preserve the natural area. Sometimes refered to as "packin/pack out".

Lexan: A material used in water bottles and other camping gear that is extremely durable and can withstand a wide range of temperatures.

Loft: The height and thickness of insulation in a sleeping bag.

Lumbar pad: A support on a backpack to comfort heavy loads on the lower back.

M

Magnetic north: The geographical region towards which all magnetic needles point. This point is approximately 1,300 miles south of true north.

Marquee: A large tent, often used as a dining or meeting tent.

Modified dome: A dome tent that has been designed for specific elements, such as wind or snow.

Mummy bag: A close fitting, shaped, hooded sleeping bag very efficient at conserving body heat.

N

No-see-um mesh: A tent mesh so fine that it keeps out the tiny biting bugs called no-see-ums.

Noggin: A small camper's mug.

O

Orienteering: Using a map and compass in the field to determine your route of travel.

P

Packed size: The dimensions of a collapsed tent and its contents, in square inches.

PolarGuard® 3D: A hollow-fiber, highly durable, polyester insulation used in sleeping bags and clothing that has a high warmth-to-weight ratio.

Pole sleeves: Fabric tunnels on the outside of a tent into which the tent poles are inserted.

Primaloft®: A microfibrous polyester insulation so close to down in terms of structure, warmth, and feel that it's also known as patented synthetic down. Primaloft is lightweight, durable, very compressible, and unlike down, highly water repellent.

Priming: Allowing fuel to collect in the burner of a white-gas stove before ignition.

Prismatic compass: A compass with a mirror designed to allow a user to see both distant objects being sighted and the compass face at the same time.

Puncheon: A log bridge built over fragile terrain that is wet.

Punkies: Also called no-see-ums; a tiny insect called a midge, which bites severely.

Purifier: A drinking water system that removes contaminates and eliminates viruses with a combination of specialized filters.

Q

Quilted: A stitching style that runs through the shell and lining of a sleeping bag or garment to keep insulation from shifting. Quilting is lighter and less expensive than it's more complex cousin, baffle construction. It is also less efficient because the stitching compresses the loft out of the fabrics and allows cold to move freely through the compressed area around the needle holes.

R

Rain fly: A tent covering that aids in keeping a tent dry and windproof.

Rating: The degree Fahrenheit to which a sleeping bag is constructed to sleep comfortably. i.e. -30 degrees, 0 degrees, +15 degrees.

Rucksack: A type of knapsack or backpack, usually made of canvas with two shoulder straps.

S

S'Mores: Popular camping dessert, consisting of chocolate bars and toasted marshmallows sandwiched between graham crackers.

Seam tape: A waterproof tape applied over all seams on a tent or other equipment meant to be totally water repellent.

Shell: The outermost material in a sleeping bag or outdoor clothing, consisting of a fabric used to meet a particular demand such as abrasion resistance, water repellency or suppleness.

Shock cord: An elastic cord running through tent poles to separation or loss of the poles, and to expedite set-up.

Single-walled tent: A lightweight, single-fabric construction tent that is chemically treated for insulation and waterproofness but which may not be very breathable.

Snow stakes: Wide, platform-type stakes used to anchor a 4-season tent in snow.

Stay: The backbone of aluminum or plastic material supporting an internal frame backpack.

Stile: A structure built over a fence that allows hikers to cross over without having to deal with a gate.

Switchback: A zigzagging trail up the side of a steep ridge, hill or mountain, which allows for a more gradual and less strenuous ascent.

T

Tent Pad: An area at a campground site designed for tent set up. Tent pads are usually covered in sand, cement or small gravel.

Three-season tent: A tent recommended for use in summer, spring, and fall.

Topographical map: A map that identifies land features (topography), as well as roads and man-made structures.

Trailhead: The place where a trail, or multiple trails begin.

Tread: A trail's surface.

Tumpline: A strap across the forehead and over the shoulders, used to carry loads on the back.

Tunnel tent: A low profile tent that is long and rounded.

U

Ultralight tent (Camping): A tent designed for one or two people, weighing five pounds or less and designed to carry on or in a backpack.

UV degradation (Camping): A breaking down of material due to the sun's harsh ultraviolet rays. UV degradation can be a potential problem with tent flies exposed to the sun for extended periods.

V

Vestibule: A covered area outside of or connected to a tent, usually created by an extended rain-fly or a special attachment.

Volume: The amount of space in a backpack measured in cubic inches.

WORKS CITED

Andrea. "Spring Camping: The Ultimate List of Tips, Essentials, and Destinations - Embracing the Wind." - *Embracing the Wind*, 2022, https://embracingthewind. com/spring-camping-tips/. Accessed 11 January 2022.

All Receipes. "Simple Grilled Lamb Chops Recipe." *Allrecipes*, 2022, https://www.allrecipes.com/rec- ipe/137917/simple-grilled-lamb-chops/. Accessed 24 January 2022.

Boogman, Saskia. "Fresh Data Indicates Camping Interest To Remain High In 2021." *PR Newswire*, 21 April 2021, https://www.prnewswire.com/ news-releases/fresh-data-indicates-camping-interes t-to-remain-high-in-2021-301273611.html. Accessed 9 January 2022.

Camping Maniacs. "Step By Step Guide on How to Set Up a Tent (Like a Pro!)." *Camping Maniacs*, 2022, https:// www.campingmaniacs.com/how-to-set-up-a-tent. Accessed 9 January 2022.

"Camp Kitchen Checklist." *REI*, https://www.rei.com/learn/ expert-advice/camp-kitchen-checklist.html. Accessed 13 January 2022.

Carroll, Ian. "How to pick the best camping knife." *Outdoor Revival*, 3 January 2018, https://

www.outdoorrevival.com/kit-and-equipment/ how-to-pick-best-camping-knife.html. Accessed 23 February 2022.

Giralt, Steve. "Perfectly Grilled Steak Recipe | Bobby Flay." *Food Network*, 2022, https://www.foodnetwork.com/recipes/bobby-flay/perfectly-grilled-steak-recipe-1973350. Accessed 24 January 2022.

Gould, Amanda. "No-oven pizza recipe." *BBC Good Food*, 7 January 2014, https://www.bbcgoodfood.com/recipes/ no-oven-pizza. Accessed 26 January 2022.

Greatist. "Camp Cooking 101: Tips, Hacks, and How-To." *Greatist*, 25 October 2021, https://greatist.com/eat/ camping-food-guide-ideas#Keep-It-Clean. Accessed 18 January 2022.

James, Jim. "Do Campfires Attract or Repel Wild Animals? How Do You Avoid Them?" *Survival Freedom*, 10 January 2022, https://survivalfreedom.com/do-campfire s-attract-or-repel-wild-animals-how-do-you-a void-them/. Accessed 13 January 2022.

Jenott, Logan. "How to Choose Knives & Multi-Tools." *REI*, 2021, https://www.rei.com/learn/expert-advice/ knives-and-tools—how-to-choose.html. Accessed 23 February 2022.

KOA. "2020 NORTH AMERICAN CAMPING REPORT: INCLUDING UPDATES." *2020 NORTH AMERICAN CAMPING REPORT: INCLUDING UPDATES*, 2020, https://ownakoa.com/2020/10/13/2020-north-american-camping-report-including-updates/. Accessed 13 1 2022.

Mann, Susan Box. "14 Best Campfire Stories (Scary / Funny / Creepy)." *IcebreakerIdeas*, 16 April 2019, https://

icebreakerideas.com/campfire-stories/. Accessed 26 January 2022.

Nellies Free range. "Muffin Pan Eggs on the Grill Recipe." *Nellie's Free Range*, 2022, https://www.nelliesfreerange. com/egg-recipes/muffin-pan-eggs-grill. Accessed 24 January 2022.

NEMO. "8 Best Beach Camping Tips." *NEMO Equipment*, 20 June 2017, https://www.nemoequip-ment.com/8-best-beach-camping-tips/. Accessed 23 February 2022.

OutdoorIndustry, KOA, Forbes. "70+ Camping Statistics (2020-2021): Industry Trends." *Condor Ferries*, 2021, https://www.condorferries.co.uk/camping-statistics. Accessed 9 January 2022.

Pantenburg, Leon. "Video: How to find dry firemak-ing tinder in wet weather." *Survival Common Sense*, 21 November 2020, https://survivalcommonsense. com/find-dry-tinder-in-wet-weather/. Accessed 18 January 2022.

Rees Enterprises LLC. "Internet While Camping: 8 Ways to Get Wi-Fi – Van Camping Life." *Van Camping Life*, 2022, https://vancampinglife.com/internet-whil e-camping-8-ways-to-get-wi-fi/. Accessed 17 January 2022.

REI. "Backpacking Clothes: What to Wear Backpacking." *REI*, 2022, https://www.rei.com/learn/expert-advice/ backpacking-clothes.html. Accessed 17 January 2022.

REI. "Camping & Emergency Lanterns: How to Choose." *REI*, 2022, https://www.rei.com/learn/expert-advice/lan-tern.html. Accessed 10 March 2022.

REI. "Sleeping Bags for Camping: How to Choose." *REI*, 2022, https://www.rei.com/learn/expert-advice/ sleeping-bag.html. Accessed 17 January 2022.

ReserveAmerica. "Top 10 Tips for Campfire Safety." *Reserve America*, 8 July 2021, https://www.reserveamerica. com/articles/camping/top-10-tips-for-campfire-safety. Accessed 18 January 2022.

Rudo, . "4 Questions To Ask When Choosing Hiking Boots." *The Foot Hub*, 12 March 2018, https://thefoothub.com.au/4-questions-to-as k-when-choosing-hiking-boots/. Accessed 8 January 2022.

Shane, Outdoor. "What Is the Best Tent Color? – Outdoor Know How." *Outdoor Know How*, 12 October 2020, https://outdoorknowhow.com/ what-is-the-best-tent-color/. Accessed 12 January 2022.

Stapleton, Valerie Loughney. "Sleeping Pads & Camping Mats: How to Choose." *REI*, 2022, https://www.rei.com/ learn/expert-advice/sleeping-pads.html. Accessed 25 February 2022.

Stewart, Martha. "Campfire Chicken Under a Brick with Lemons Recipe." *Martha Stewart*, 2022, https://www.marthastewart.com/354917/ campfire-chicken-under-brick-lemons. Accessed 25 January 2022.

Verma, Sonali Anand. "Camping Terminology and Words You Should Know | Bass Pro Shops." *Bass Pro Shops 1Source*, 14 May 2013, https://1source. basspro.com/news-tips/camping-information/7565/ camping-terminology-and-words-you-should-know. Accessed 17 January 2022.

Wildeck, Tyler. "15 Unexpected Benefits of Camping
for Your Health and Happiness." *The Dyrt*, 26
March 2019, https://thedyrt.com/magazine/life-
style/unexpected-benefits-of-camping/. Accessed 13
January 2022.

Woodruff, Scott. "15 Awesome Summer Camping
Tips | Summer Camping Hacks." *Tents n
Trees*, 19 February 2021, https://tentsntrees.
com/15-awesome-summer-camping-tips/. Accessed 9
January 2022.

Made in United States
Orlando, FL
31 March 2022

16344233R00102